Behavioral Sciences in
Secondary Schools

THE PROFESSIONAL EDUCATION SERIES

Walter K. Beggs, *Editor*
Dean Emeritus
Teachers College
University of Nebraska

Royce H. Knapp, *Research Editor*
Regents Professor of Education
Teachers College
University of Nebraska

Behavioral Sciences in Secondary Schools

by

RANDALL C. ANDERSON

Professor of Social Sciences
and Social Science Education
Emporia Kansas State College

PROFESSIONAL EDUCATORS PUBLICATIONS, INC.
LINCOLN, NEBRASKA

Library of Congress Catalog Card No.: 75-9148

ISBN   0-88224-098-6

1|5|79 Beeber + Tyler 2.25

Contents

CHAPTER 1

Introduction to the Behavioral Sciences

In comparison to the traditional social science disciplines of history, geography, economics, and political science, the behavioral science subject areas are relatively new to junior and senior high school social studies programs, as well as to the curricular structure of most colleges and universities. This is not to imply that the disciplines which comprise the behavioral sciences are new to the academic community. Throughout most of the twentieth century, many major institutions of higher education in the United States have provided some offerings in the three primary disciplines comprising the behavioral sciences: sociology, social psychology, and cultural anthropology. During this period, however, few colleges and universities referred to these disciplines as the "behavioral sciences," offered undergraduate or graduate majors in the "behavioral sciences," or had administrative units known as departments of "behavioral sciences."[1]

This situation, however, is no longer the case. There exists little doubt that full-fledged programs in the behavioral sciences are, currently, among the most rapidly expanding academic and professional curricula in most colleges and universities in the nation, on both the undergraduate and graduate levels. Furthermore, all available evidence would indicate that programs, instructional faculties, and administrative departments in the behavioral sciences will continue to expand at a most rapid rate on college and university campuses throughout the remainder of the present century and well into the twenty-first century. The professional literature of higher education, as well as budget appropriations for academic innovation and expansion in higher education, substantiates this conclusion.

THE RATIONALE FOR THE BEHAVIORAL SCIENCES

Both the academic disciplines which comprise the behavioral sciences and the behavioral sciences field (which, in some instances, is presently being referred to as the "life sciences") will continue to be a most significant component in American education. By the mid-twentieth century, it had become obvious to influential educational leaders that the major concerns of formal education and research in the United States must be directed toward improving the quality of human life and society. The century-long emphasis upon industrialization and highly sophisticated technology continued to result in an ever-increasing rate of societal ills, divisiveness, militarism, and human tragedy. In essence, the price paid for becoming the world's most technologically advanced nation was a set of individual and collective human problems which were plaguing American society at an alarming rate.

The individual and group anxiety-producing problems which American society is now experiencing will be with us during the foreseeable future. Indeed, it is clear that society must continue to support the institutions which can help alleviate these areas of concern. Technological advancement and knowledge now involve issues of life and death, issues that will continue to significantly influence the quality and quantity of life. Science and technology alone will not solve our social problems. Emphasis must now be placed upon institutions that will place a priority upon improving the human condition within our society, which is becoming ever-increasingly complex.[2]

Other than the family, the major social agent for the accomplishment of these goals is the system of formal education. Within the educational structure, the primary responsibility for promoting positive societal change has become the realm of the academic disciplines comprising the behavioral sciences.

THE SOCIAL SCIENCES AND THE BEHAVIORAL SCIENCES

As an area of academic investigation, the behavioral science field is relatively new to American higher education. The term *behavioral science* achieved widespread prominence as an academic phrase during the early 1950s, when the influential Ford Foundation gave financial support to develop a nationwide program on individual behavior and human relations. In the mid-1950s the Ford Foundation termed this project the Behavioral Sciences Program.[3]

With the advent of the behavioral science field, there immediately arose questions from many within the academic community concerning the distinctions between the traditional social sciences and the emerging behavioral sciences. For purposes of clarification, the term *social sciences* is usually considered to include seven academic disciplines: anthropology, economics, geography, history, political science, psychology, and sociology. In reality, human affairs are so complex that academic categories, however carefully delimited, cannot contain them neatly. For example, the social sciences commonly shares one of its member disciplines, history, with the humanities; another, psychology, with the biological sciences; and anthropology with both. In addition, in many instances, other social science disciplines, such as economics and political science, are included within professional schools of business and public administration, respectively.

The behavioral sciences focus on three of the social science disciplines. Comprising the core of the behavioral sciences are the American versions of anthropology, psychology, and sociology.[4] There is an inherent difference between the behavioral sciences on the one hand and the social sciences on the other. Since their inception, the disciplines comprising the behavioral sciences have typically been more devoted to the investigation and collection of original data reflecting the direct behavior of individuals and groups than to the more aggregate, indirect, and documentary research methodologies employed by economists, political scientists, and historians.

To be considered a component of the behavioral sciences field, therefore, a discipline must satisfy two fundamental criteria. First, it must emphasize the study of human behavioral patterns. Second, it must analyze its subject matter in a scientific manner. The immediate scientific objective is one of establishing valid generalizations about human behavior that are supported by empirical evidence gathered in an objective and impersonal way. The ultimate objective of research in the behavioral sciences is to comprehend, explain, and predict human behavior in the same sense in which scientists understand, explain, and predict the behavior of physical and biological phenomena.[5] In addition, social studies teachers should be aware of the continued debate that exists among some social and behavioral scientists as to whether or not scientific research methods can be applied to the study of many characteristics of human behavior.

Obviously, the academic boundaries of such a broad concept as the behavioral sciences cannot be specifically defined. The academic profession continues to waste considerable time and energy debating whether some element of the human condition is or is not properly included within the behavioral sciences. The basis of the concept would seem to be relatively clear. Indeed, the term *behavioral sciences* does not appear to be less precise or more misleading than the term *social sciences,* which traditionally has not included some fields that also might claim to be either "social" or "sciences" in scope and purpose. In essence, it is not particularly useful to argue over the definitions of academic areas in an attempt to clarify every conceivable misconception, interpretation, exception, or assumed contradiction. Such questions cannot be answered specifically in every instance, nor is there any compelling academic reason why they must be.

The Concept of Culture

An additional basic reason for considering the disciplines of sociology, social psychology, and cultural anthropology as behavioral sciences and, thus, apart from the traditional social science disciplines of history, economics, political science, and geography, is that the central theme of each of the behavioral disciplines is "culture," a concept so significant but so broad and all-inclusive that it is nearly beyond comprehension in all of its ramifications. One means of achieving some understanding of culture is to learn how it began and developed. Culture, as we are experiencing it in the latter decades of the twentieth century, is the result of over a million years of mankind on earth and the dissemination of what mankind has learned. Of vital importance to the culture concept is the theory that personal behavior is learned from group settings and that it is not inherent or biological in the individual. A prerequisite to individual cultural traits or characteristics, therefore, is group interaction. Culture and cultural traditions are learned by the individual from the group and are continuous as a result of being transmitted from generation to generation.[6]

The significance of culture as treated by the behavioral science disciplines of sociology, social psychology, and cultural anthropology is that, unlike the traditional social science disciplines of history, economics, political science, and geography, the first three disciplines place priority upon investigating the "general" sciences of man, whereas the latter subjects of economics, political science, and geography are considered "special" sciences. For instance, the political scientist considers only the political process and political institutions; the geographer emphasizes the study of the interrelationships between man and his environment; whereas the sociologist, the social psychologist, and the cultural anthropologist are concerned with the totality of social institutions and behavior—religious, familial, sexual, legal, educational, economic, and so on. The major reason for these wide parameters of study is that the sociologist and the anthropologist are continually striving to discover concepts or principles applicable to group or social organization in an attempt to determine the reasons for certain types of group and, thereby, individual behavioral patterns. Although history, as an academic discipline, is also an interpretive or general subject, it is unique because of its descriptive consideration of particular movements and events. Both in teaching and research, however, such formal disciplinary distinctions cannot be observed in many instances; thus, practitioners who consider themselves sociologists, anthropologists, or social psychologists often investigate social problems which have overlapping boundaries.[7]

DEFINING THE BEHAVIORAL SCIENCES

As an academic field of study, the behavioral sciences are now well established in higher education. During recent decades, the disciplines comprising this field of investigation have contributed significantly to our understanding of man and society. Such indispensable contributions will continue to be forthcoming. The behavioral sciences must be considered one of the major intellectual creations of the twentieth century.

The objectives of the individual behavioral science disciplines are essentially the same as those of the other sciences: to establish a body of fact and theory that contributes to the knowledge and understanding that will permit humanity to manage its affairs with continually greater rationality.

Cultural Anthropology

The discipline of cultural anthropology cuts across the academic boundaries which separate the natural sciences from the social sciences and encompasses both areas within its spectrum. An additional unique characteristic of cultural anthropology is that it represents the newest discipline of the behavioral sciences to be developed.[8] Cultural anthropology historically has been concerned with the organization, institutional arrangements, belief systems, and the general manner of life of rather small and isolated groups of people, usually referred to as nonliterate because they possess no written records. Studies of an American Indian pueblo, a tribe of Australian aborigines, or a group living in the interior highlands of New Guinea are typical. During recent years, the research methods of cultural anthropology have extended to the investigation of small human settlements in close proximity to major urban areas, and to such problems as kinship structure in more highly developed communities.[9] One of the most recent movements in the area of cultural anthropology is that professional anthropologists are concentrating their attention more and more on the study of technologically advanced and semiadvanced societies within the context of increasing societal complexity.[10]

Since anthropology is the field of investigation which is concerned not only with the study of the evolution of man and his works but also with the ways in which these have influenced change in man and his works, it should be obvious that there are few disciplines more revealing of the nature of man and the societies which he has evolved. Cultural anthropology attempts to better understand the great variety of human ethnic groups and their societies. As such, cultural anthropology can be considered to be the science of cultural differences and similarities on a global basis.

Most of the important social issues confronting modern societies today are easy to identify. A general enumeration would include overpopulation, environmental pollution, crime and violence, juvenile delinquency, poverty, racism in all its forms, including ideas of inherently superior and inferior races, political overcontrol, war, drug abuse, mental illness, and so on. The investigation of these issues from the perspective of different cultural groups, with the hope of offering solutions to the major behavioral problems of societies, is the central role of modern cultural anthropology as a behavioral science discipline.

Social Psychology

The predictability of another individual's behavior, particularly someone we care about or depend upon, is an important characteristic of human life. This situation causes us to develop certain "expectancies" regarding one another's behavior, based upon past experiences. Obviously, the fulfillment of such expectancies is a vital element in explaining social behavior.

Social psychology is one of the scientific fields concerned with the objective investigation of human behavior. The behavioral emphasis in psychology has resulted in the establishment of many laboratories for the study of brain-behavior relationships. There the techniques of neuroanatomy, neurochemistry, and neurophysiology are used, together with the special kinds of equipment that psychologists have developed for exploring their interests in sensory and cognitive processes, in learning, memory, motivation, and behavioral genetics.[11] Specifically, the social psychologist directs his investigations toward achieving a better understanding of the influences which produce regularities and diversities in human social behavior. Social psychology's particular role is the result of two major factors: first, the discipline's interest in the individual as an active participant in social relationships; and, second, its emphasis on understanding the social influence processes which determine these relationships. In an attempt to achieve a systematic comprehension of social behavior, social psychologists strive to obtain evidence from experimentation regarding their predictions about social influences upon individuals.

The primary concern of social psychology, therefore, is with the process of social influence upon people. Obviously, humans are oriented by economic and personal motives toward other humans within their societal environment, and social influence occurs whenever an individual responds to the actual or implied presence of one or more other persons. In essence, most of the characteristics all individuals possess are influenced by social interaction, including personality and related values and attitudes. As an academic discipline, social psychology is also concerned with the wider range of influence relationships that prevail between a group and an individual, such as prejudice, social conformity, morale, leadership, and other phenomena.

Social psychology's unique responsibility as one of the behavioral sciences can best be summarized by stating sample questions which the social psychologist attempts to answer as he investigates group influences upon individual behavior:

1. What are the group influences which cause individual attitudes and value systems to change?
2. What are the conditions which will cause certain individuals to act independently of a particular group?
3. What are the consequences of a conflict of values dictated by different groups with which an individual is identified?[12]

The major function of social psychology as a behavioral science, and, therefore, as a discipline which can contribute to the solution of many social problems, is its investigation of the psychology of the individual in society. Thus, the subject's main objective is to attempt to determine the influences of the social environment upon the personal behavior of individuals.

Sociology

The field of sociology in the United States developed as the result of a social experience which had very little to do with the political and ideological controversies that stimulated sociology in France and Germany. Rather, the discipline evolved as a result of the experiences associated with the problems of an immigrant society caught in the turmoil of rapid industrialization and urban growth. Indeed, it must be emphasized that from its beginnings, sociology has had a very practical interest, which was characterized less by political divisiveness than by social reform and social work. This practical emphasis in the discipline has continued to persist to the present. It has only been since World War II, however, that there has existed something in American higher education that could be properly termed a "sociological establishment" or a highly respected academic field of study.[13] Its major strength as an academic discipline resulted from its empirical and sophisticated approach to the identification and solution of practical but highly significant social problems.

Today, what does the academic sociologist do? Professional sociologists are individuals who study and teach about societies, social institutions, and the patterns of human interaction and human behavior. As a scientific discipline, sociology may be divided into three broad, analytical fields: the study of groups; institutional analysis; and the study of the social structure in general.[14] Thus, the content of the rapidly expanding discipline of sociology is based upon culture and society, with emphasis placed upon the study of the various types of interaction and relationships which exist among individuals and human groups. In the study of such areas as social organization and disorganization, sociologists attempt to explain the evolution and change of social institutions and the changing nature of human attitudinal and value systems. Among the selected topics of investigation included within the study of sociology are the changing nature of family life, institutional life, sexual attitudes, crime and violence, religious values, and the entire gamut of interpersonal relationships in politics and government. Indeed, many of the areas which professional sociologists study are, by their very nature, relatively familiar to many of us even though they are not clearly understood. The basic hypotheses of the discipline—that social life (both group and individual behavior) is patterned; that values and attitudes are learned, reinforced, and shared; that we as individuals are, in many respects, what others consider us to be—are ideas which most people now instinctively accept in order to live and function as members of society. These topics, which emphasize individual and group behavior processes, then, comprise the areas of concern for sociology as one of the behavioral science disciplines.

During these last decades of the twentieth century, advanced Western society will continue to be confronted with crucial social issues in the context of both individual and group behavior patterns resulting from continued rapid technological expansion. The solutions to the problems plaguing our complex society will become, to a much greater extent, the primary responsibility of sociology, social psychology, and cultural anthropology, the three major academic disciplines comprising the behavioral sciences. This trend is being witnessed currently by the increasing numbers of behavioral scientists that are being employed by government, by business and industry, by hospitals and other agencies devoted to problems of health care, by welfare agencies, by public educational systems, and by many other types of organizations in which some systematic knowledge of human behavior is required.

CHAPTER 2

The Behavioral Sciences and the
Social Studies Curriculum

Of all the subject areas comprising the junior and senior high school curriculum, the social studies program is the field most directly responsible for achieving the objectives of education in a democratic society. Specifically, the foremost role of the social studies curriculum is the transmission of values, attitudes, ideals, and elements of the cultural heritage to the nation's youth for the ultimate purpose of producing "democratic citizens."[1] According to the traditional interpretation of this thesis, the social studies program is more directly involved than any other subject-matter area in the development and perpetuation of strong feelings of loyalty and patriotism among the nation's populace and, thus, a high degree of national viability and political cohesion. Indeed, the view that the inculcation of citizenship education based upon a high degree of nationalism should remain as the primary rationale for social studies instruction continues to be a basic premise of some influential educators and lay groups throughout the nation. Obviously, however, many educators expound a much broader view of the basic objectives of the social studies in the contemporary American education system.

THE CHANGING RATIONALE FOR CITIZENSHIP EDUCATION

Paralleling the "nationalistic" objective for social studies education is the very common professional as well as public definition of democratic citizenship, which is widely referred to as worthy membership in American society. According to this widely held view, an individual's contributions to society, the manner in which he respects or fails to respect the rights and values of others, and even the attitudes he instills within his children, have significant implications for the community and, thus, the nation.[2] Thus, any curriculum which contributes to the physical, emotional, social, and moral development of youth contributes directly to the welfare of the nation and should be considered the foremost goal of education for democratic citizenship. This premise holds that citizenship education in the social studies curriculum should be indistinguishable from those human traits which contribute positively to the welfare of society.

8

Social Studies and the Social Order

Since the developmental era in American precollegiate education, the secondary social studies curriculum has placed emphasis upon the transmission of knowledge and skills derived from the academic social and behavioral science disciplines. It should be noted at this point that the social science disciplines are separate and systematic fields of study whose content is organized around social, cultural, economic, and political relationships and behavior. Each of the social sciences possesses a method of research or inquiry to continually investigate human and social phenomena and, thus, create new knowledge for the various disciplines. The social studies in the secondary school curriculum are distinguishable from the social science disciplines in higher education in the following four basic respects: (1) scope, (2) size, (3) purpose, and (4) level of difficulty. In both scope and size, the academic social sciences are much more extensive than the social studies.[3] The purpose of the academic social scientist is to search out and contribute new knowledge to his discipline. The objective of the social studies teacher is to direct students in their learning of selected segments of what social scientists have investigated and discovered. The social studies instructor, therefore, selects content based upon the research of social scientists and develops innovative techniques for translating it into comprehensible material for the secondary student. Regardless of the particular course title, the subject materials comprising the social studies program are usually of an integrated nature, drawing upon the content of several of the social science disciplines.

Throughout the contemporary period, social studies instruction in the secondary schools has been concerned almost entirely with the promulgation of right or wrong answers and with the accumulation of descriptive facts, largely in the abstract and divorced from the student's social environment. At an ever-increasing rate, however, influential social studies educators are professing the belief that the primary rationale for the social studies program should be to better prepare students to function productively in a complex and constantly changing domestic and international society. In addition, these educational leaders are currently expressing the view that the social studies program must place priority upon promoting a more realistic awareness of the many urgent human and social problems confronting the nation, and should better equip today's students to become actively engaged in their solution. In order to successfully accomplish these goals, it is vital that considerably more emphasis be placed upon the integration of materials and methodologies from the behavioral sciences in the social studies curriculum.

Since the inception of the contemporary social studies curriculum, as endorsed in 1916 by the Committee on Social Studies appointed by the National Education Association,[4] the vast majority of youth has had no opportunity to become acquainted with the behavioral sciences and, consequently, has had virtually no opportunity for reflective inquiry into the nature of the individual and group behavioral characteristics that are both the result and the cause of many of the highly complex social problems presently confronting our nation. Indeed, until only very recently, anthropology, psychology, and sociology were not offered, either as separate or integrated courses on either a required or an elective basis, in the American precollegiate curricular structure.

The Behavioral Sciences and Social Studies

By the mid-1970s, however, there is no doubt that the behavioral sciences are increasing in importance in the secondary social studies curriculum. Furthermore, the traditional subjects of history, geography, and government will continue to be challenged by the emerging fields of sociology, social psychology, and cultural anthropology, which emphasize the consideration of human behavioral patterns in both individual and group contexts. Since the social studies draw upon the literature of the academic social and behavioral sciences, it is also highly probable that even if separate courses are not offered in one or more of the subjects comprising the behavioral sciences, the content and method of sociology, social psychology, and cultural anthropology will constitute a most important interdisciplinary component of the social studies curriculum within the near future. The academic behavioral science disciplines have developed methodologies and approaches for the study of individual and group social problems which will significantly influence the content and methods of the more traditional social studies subjects, such as government and economics, which have traditionally had a historical basis.[5] Not only government, economics, and geography, but also courses in United States and world history, will integrate more and more of the content and methodology of the three behavioral science subject fields.

The Behavioral Sciences in Secondary Social Studies

The relationships between the elementary and secondary social studies and the academic social and behavioral sciences are oftentimes confusing to both in-service and pre-service teachers, as well as to parents and other individuals unfamiliar with the literature of professional education. However, controversies involving the recognized distinctions between the terms *social sciences, behavioral sciences,* and *social studies* are irrelevant in view of the conscientious thought that is currently being given to the consideration of what new and innovative strategies to implement in secondary social studies. With regard to the problem of selecting content from the academic behavioral science disciplines which can be translated into comprehensible materials for secondary students, the following statements may be considered as working definitions for those teachers and students responsible for social studies curriculum design:

Cultural Anthropology.   Cultural anthropology in secondary education is the study of different ethnic and racial groups—their cultural traditions, customs, life-styles, social mores, and languages—existing in various global regions in different historical periods. While placing priority upon the examination of modern cultures, the emphasis of anthropological study at the secondary level should be on the analysis and explanation of why world cultures differ from one another.

Since cultural anthropology is the newest of the behavioral sciences to be included within the secondary social studies curriculum, its content and method are most frequently integrated into existing courses, such as sociology, social psychology, geography, world history, and world cultures.

Social Psychology. In the social studies program, this subject should prepare students to comprehend more adequately the influencing factors which contribute to the behavioral patterns of individuals and groups. Thus, both the psychological and physiological aspects of personal and societal behavior, as well as human motivational traits, should be incorporated into any systematic examination of social psychology.

Like cultural anthropology, social psychology is one of the newer behavioral sciences to be introduced into the secondary schools. Thus, the subject-matter topics and the unique mode of inquiry from this discipline are most commonly found within the boundaries of more established social studies subjects rather than as a distinct course offering.

Sociology. Closely related to both cultural anthropology and social psychology, sociology is the most established behavioral science discipline in the social studies program as a separate course offering, and in addition is the most rapidly expanding subject area in the social studies curriculum.

The content and method of sociology in social education includes culture and society, with emphasis placed upon the study of the various types of interaction and relationships which exist among individuals and groups. In their investigation of social organization and disorganization, sociologists attempt to explain the evolution and change of social institutions and the changing nature of attitudinal and value systems. Thus, the changing nature of family life, institutional life, sexual attitudes, crime and violence, religious values, and the interpersonal relationships in politics and government are among the topics included within the study of sociology in the secondary social studies.

These represent the behavioral sciences subject areas which are rapidly emerging in the secondary social studies curriculum. The increasing significance of these subjects as a major component in social education is due to the fact that their content and methodology are concerned more directly with individual and group behavioral patterns than the traditional social studies subjects of history, geography, economics, and government. As a result, they place more emphasis upon promoting student awareness of both the problems and the possible solutions to many of the crucial social issues confronting American society today.

Introducing Behavioral Science Research Methods

As the behavioral sciences attain greater significance in the social studies curriculum, it is important that students achieve a basic understanding of the methodologies, or modes of inquiry, employed by professional anthropologists, psychologists, and sociologists in their research and investigation of particular individual and group behavioral patterns. When students have achieved some level of understanding concerning the methods of investigation utilized by the behavioral sciences, they should be aware of some of the primary differences in the research techniques used by behavioral scientists and other social scientists, such as historians or geographers. For instance, the mode of inquiry employed in historical research emphasizes the interpretive analysis of original documents in the study of contemporary or past events, and is based upon the validity— positive affirmation or negative affirmation—of the particular documentary evidence under consideration. Geographical research, on the other hand, utilizes methods of field observations to examine changes in particular regions through time and to study the impact of the natural and cultural environments upon regional change. After students are familiar with behavioral science research methods, individuals or groups of students can be directed to carry out independent research projects which will reinforce their understanding both of human behavior and of the methods of investigation used by academic behavioral scientists.

There are three basic research designs utilized by behavioral scientists in their study of individual and group behavioral characteristics: the experiment, the survey, and the case study.[6]

The Experiment. The experimental research method is defined as any investigation that includes two elements: the control of some variable by the researcher, and the systematic observation of the result. Specifically, this means that there is active intervention on the phenomenon under examination to see what, if any, changes result from the intervention. Behavioral scientists can increase their knowledge of mental disease and emotional illness by means of physiological intervention in the human nervous system accompanied by controlled observation of the behavioral results. For example, psychologists could examine the effects of administering several types of tranquilizers to different individuals over various time periods. Many studies have been undertaken to determine the changes in human behavior resulting from different types of chemical intervention.[7]

Practical considerations, however, make the experimental research design relatively difficult for use in secondary schools. Such sophisticated studies require an understanding of statistical methods which are unfamiliar to most students. Furthermore, few secondary schools possess the physical facilities, such as well-equipped laboratories, in which students can work with animals under the proper investigative conditions. Nevertheless, the observations of behavioral scientists can be made available so that students will have the opportunity to examine both the method of investigation and the results of the research.

The Sample Survey. A second research technique employed by the behavioral scientist is known as the sample survey. The sample survey also contains two elements, the sample and the survey. To the researcher, the sample represents the particular group, or "population," he is interested in investigating (such as high school students, college students, black voters, elementary teachers, etc.). There are several types of samples, such as "random," "representative," "quota," and "weighted."[8] The major principle for student awareness is that the investigator selects the sample in such a manner that he can draw conclusions regarding the entire population, and not only the members of the population who are included in the sample.

The survey represents the information, or data, collected from the particular population under examination. For instance, the individuals in the sample could be asked such questions as their attitudes toward legalized abortion, premarital sex, euthanasia, diplomatic relations with the People's Republic of China, etc. In addition to determining magnitude, such as how many people in a sample favor increased social security benefits, sample surveys provide additional information. For example, a survey of numbers of children per family can provide data concerning fertility rates of families by different class structure, ethnic groups, regional location, rural-urban residence, and so on.

However, conducting surveys also poses certain problems for public school systems. The administrations of many schools frown upon the practice of encouraging students to interview citizens in the community. In a number of schools students have designed survey instruments and administered them to groups within the confines of the school. This strategy has great potential. Students can also be provided with survey instruments and data to examine which have been designed and collected by professional behavioral scientists.

The Case Study. The case study is somewhat similar to the sample survey. However, while the survey method measures a few characteristics of many people over a short time period, the case study procedure examines many characteristics of one particular phenomenon, such as a culture group, a specific global region, an urban area, a small town, an individual, etc,. over a long time span. The purpose of the case study method is to gain as much knowledge as possible about the one case under study. Typical case studies in the behavioral sciences might include: the life history of an alcoholic or a drug addict, an intensive analysis of a certain type of criminal offender, a detailed anthropological study describing the values, attitudes, customs, and technological progress of a particular culture group, or an intensive study of a Chinese commune. Unlike many research problems in the behavioral sciences, the case study does not commonly involve the attempt to prove or disprove a hypothesis or an assumption.[9] Rather, it provides a vast reservoir of knowledge concerning a particular phenomenon.

By far the largest amount of data available for use in the study of sociology, social psychology, and anthropology in secondary school social studies is provided by case studies. Behavioral scientists representing these disciplines have contributed thousands of articles describing cases they have studied, ranging from individual behavior patterns to investigations of culture groups in both primitive and technologically advanced societies. These articles can be used in nearly any social studies class. Most significantly, they are a particularly valuable source of subject data and an excellent means of introducing students to the scientific mode of inquiry used by the behavioral scientist.

THE BEHAVIORAL SCIENCES AND CURRICULUM DESIGN

The more precollegiate education in the United States becomes a concern of public or social welfare, and the more it becomes an issue of public debate and policy-making, the more the educational sector will be expected to utilize its resources in an attempt to solve the many serious social problems of the contemporary period. As previously implied, of all the subject areas comprising the secondary school curriculum, the social studies program is the curricular area that is the most synonymous with the ultimate objectives and goals of the American educational system, since it has the direct responsibility for preparing the nation's youth to live and function positively as adult citizens in a democratic society. In addition, secondary students of the social sciences continue to be critical of traditional educational programs. A prevalent criticism by students is the complaint that the social studies curriculum lacks relevance in relation to the social issues and events confronting mankind. These two major forces—increasing public influence from all segments of society in determining educational policies and programs, together with student concerns about curricular relevance —would appear to insure that the subjects comprising the behavioral sciences will gain substantially in prestige, as well as become major components of the social studies program on both an elective and a required basis, during the last decades of the present century.

The very positive future role of the behavioral science subjects, particularly sociology and social psychology, in the social studies program, has been further enhanced by the preparation, publication, and national dissemination of the highly influential document entitled "Social Studies Curriculum Guidelines,"[10] developed by the Task Force on Curriculum Guidelines commissioned by the National Council for the Social Studies. Contained within this document is a major section referred to as the "Basic Rationale for Social Studies Education."[11] While including the transmission of knowledge and knowledge-related skills as important components of social studies education, the statement draws the following significant conclusions concerning the role of knowledge in the contemporary social studies program:

As knowledge without action is impotent, so action without knowledge is reprehensible. Those who seek to resolve social issues without concomitant understanding tend not only to behave irresponsibly and erratically but in ways that damage their own future and the human condition. Therefore, knowledge, reason, commitment to human dignity, and action are to be regarded as complementary and inseparable.[12]

Regarding the traditional methodological and subject-matter approaches for imparting knowledge in social education, the report states:

From its inception the school has been viewed as the social institution charged with transmitting knowledge to the young. Yet, despite this longstanding responsibility, it would be difficult to demonstrate that the school has handled this task well or that standards of accuracy and validity have been systematically applied to the information presented in the classroom. Nor can many schools assert that their curricula deal effectively with significant and powerful ideas.[13]

Continuing, the statement introduces a new and significant interpretation of content knowledge in the social studies curriculum:

Furthermore, the knowledge utilized by the school has reflected the biases of the white middle class and has distorted the role of minority groups. Such distortions have prevented white people as well as members of minority groups from fully knowing themselves and their culture. Such practices are clearly inconsistent with the requirements of individuals in an increasingly complex, pluralistic society.

Knowledge about the real world and knowledge about the worthiness of personal social judgments are basic objectives of social studies instruction. . . . A major task of social studies education is to demonstrate the power of rationally-based knowledge to facilitate human survival and progress.[14]

. . . The question about appropriate sources of knowledge for social studies is indeed well-phrased in terms of the "needs" of students and society rather than the arbitrary and limiting assumption that social studies and social sciences are identical.[15]

By way of concluding the section of the statement dealing with the relation of knowledge and the contemporary social studies, the national task force perceptively observed:

In summary, the broad function of knowledge, whatever its source, is to provide the reservoir of data, ideas, concepts, generalizations, and theories which, in combination with thinking, valuing, and social participation, can be used by the student to function rationally and humanely.[16]

In addition to reinterpreting the traditional view of content knowledge and defining its primary objectives in social studies as those of promoting both a more adequate comprehension of and solutions to the nation's social problems, the NCSS Report devotes large sections to the significance of valuing abilities[17] and increased social participation[18] as major objectives of social education. The basic rationale for the inclusion of both objectives involves the importance that these concepts hold for understanding differences in individual and group attitudes and social behavior and, therefore, in the resolution of many problems confronting society.

It appears obvious that the attention afforded both increased social involvement and improving the instructional strategies for instilling valuing abilities, in conjunction with the reinterpretation of the role of knowledge, will provide a major new thrust in social studies education, in which primary goals will be reflected in efforts to prepare youth for intelligent participation in the social affairs of the nation. Divergent value judgments and attitudinal sets provide the basis of social institutions as well as individual and group behavior. Effective social involvements in a democratic society are dependent upon individual and group behavior which is determined by the values of human dignity and directed toward solving our many social problems. In terms of emphasis, American society may have realized by the late twentieth century that the correct study of man is mankind.

These new standards or guidelines, which are being included within instructional objectives for social education, will result in a great deal more emphasis being placed upon sociology, social psychology, and cultural anthropology in the social studies program. These subjects, which comprise the behavioral sciences, place priority upon understanding and solving the issues of our modern-day society since they comprise the study of human and group behavior, human attitudes and value systems, cultural traditions, various types of interaction between individuals and groups. In essence, the behavioral sciences are directly responsible for investigating the forces that are vital to social change in a pluralistic and dynamic society.

Realistically, however, the three primary behavioral science subjects will not replace the more traditional social studies course offerings in a revolutionary fashion. With regard to these traditional offerings, the trend which has already begun will gain momentum. Content and modes of inquiry from the behavioral sciences will be integrated in all social studies courses at an increasing rate. Furthermore, sociology will probably become a full-fledged separate course offering in many major secondary school systems in the near future, while social psychology will also be introduced on a separate basis in some systems. The content and methodology of cultural anthropology will most frequently be incorporated within sociology and social psychology.

All subject fields comprising the social studies program will continue to contain a significant proportion of interdisciplinary materials, regardless of the specific name attached to the course. It is conceivable that increased content integration and the establishment of more and more interdisciplinary "mini-courses" within existing offerings will render it most difficult to measure a particular subject's status on the basis of separate or required offerings in the social studies program. As noted above, the one measurable change will be the increased proportion of materials drawn from the behavioral sciences which will be introduced into the social studies curriculum. Both the expanding "crush" of knowledge now emerging in the behavioral sciences and the utilitarian educational role of behavioral science subjects render this situation inevitable. Integration and correlation of content implies no sacrifice of academic purity.[19] To the contrary, such an approach is the only possible means to acquaint secondary students with the content and methods of each of the social and behavioral science disciplines.

An exhaustive review of current professional literature and research in social studies education overwhelmingly supports the premise that a much greater degree of emphasis will continue to be placed upon the consideration of individual and group behavioral patterns within the secondary social studies curriculum throughout the foreseeable future. The complexity of the numerous contemporary social issues confronting the nation in this age of dynamic transition will necessitate this major change in the philosophy of social education.

CHAPTER 3

Social Education in the Future

Since the inception of the contemporary social studies curriculum during the second decade of the present century, the major thrust in classroom instruction has been the transmitting of subject-matter knowledge from the academic social science disciplines into content materials for secondary school youth. In the opinion of this writer, the transfer of "bits" and "chunks" of organized knowledge continues to comprise the primary "instructional process" in social studies teaching in the vast majority of instances today.

BEHAVIORAL PATTERNS AND CURRICULUM DEVELOPMENT

There currently exists a widespread feeling among educational leaders in the United States, however, that if the ultimate objectives of social studies education in a democratic society are ever to be effectively achieved, there must be a radical shift in instructional emphasis from blind obedience to the cognitive domain to a priority upon the humanization of education, a development of behavioral abilities, and a recognition of the individual as the most significant element in the complex methodology of learning. Ironically, by the decade of the 1970s, it would seem that many social studies educators have finally accepted the major thesis presented by John Dewey in his classic *The Child and the Curriculum,* published in 1902, that individual self-realization, rather than knowledge or information, is the goal of education. With regard to knowledge, Dewey maintained that it is the outgrowth or concomitant outcome of the struggle for self-realization.

In the writer's opinion, most of those who are responsible for administering and teaching in the formal educational system continue to assume that the student "inherits" the two fundamental life processes—that of physical development, controlled from within the organism; and that of mental development instilled from without, usually by parents and teachers. This false premise, which is the foundation of the outmoded "knowledge curriculum," places the individual student in a serious dilemma. In actuality, youth manage to attain their physical growth, while the educational system prevents them from openly using their life processes to meet the system's preconceived and fixed ends. Since youth's growth toward emotional self-maturity is physiological, organic wholeness cannot be satisfied by learning isolated segments of subject matter. In effect, formal education, as exemplified by so much current social studies instruction, stifles normal internal drives toward physiological wholeness to such an extent that far too many students develop an extreme dislike for "school" at an early age, become emotionally upset, lose all motivation toward seeking knowledge, reject subject matter, are considered slow learners, and frequently become disciplinary problems and dropouts. In addition, the writer believes that the more often schools introduce "innovative" techniques for teaching fragmented and irrelevant knowledge as an end in itself, the greater will be the frustration of many students.[1]

The demands of our highly complex society necessitate that the secondary social studies curriculum must in the immediate future provide the opportunities for youth to continually create their own self-realization in order that they might attain the highest level of emotional maturity possible on the basis of their individual genetic characteristics and their external physical and social environment. Social studies education must instruct youth how to achieve self-realization and emotional maturity. If this goal is to be accomplished, emphasis must be placed upon the development of individual behavior patterns which will enable youth to function productively in their social environment. The social studies program in the American educational system cannot continue to focus on the content knowledge suggested by traditional educational theorists during the height of the progressive era.[2] Indeed, if social studies instruction continues to consist almost entirely of the traditional transferal of subject matter, today's youth will become relatively less competent to cope with the uncertainties of life than were the students of previous generations, who experienced a more stable and predictable social environment. Also, so that they might successfully meet many of the problems which characterize the adolescent years, such as concern about future goals, value conflicts, physical change, alienation from family, rebellion, violence, and so on, students must be provided with a much greater opportunity to gain insights into human behavior and a more adequate comprehension of our radically changing social mores. A major thrust in social education, therefore, must be behaviorist-centered, so that the student can learn to live successfully in an ever-changing environment, realize his potential mental capabilities, and select and utilize knowledge that is beneficial to his mental and emotional growth. The priority must be shifted from the memorization of organized knowledge to the development of behavioral abilities in order that students might discover how to realize their potential in realistic terms.

Developing Behavioral Competencies

The ultimate goal of social studies instruction must be one of preparing youth to become responsible, productive, and emotionally mature individuals in a constantly changing, urbanized society. Instead of mass-producing cognitive-oriented youth capable of passively memorizing bits of information which have little, if any, relevance to the problems and alternatives which they face as adolescents and which will confront them throughout their adult lives, social studies instruction must create individuals who are able to think critically about various social problems; to apply valuing skills to particular issues and events; to develop the ability to achieve intellectual, career, and social objectives; to engage actively in social participation; and to select and utilize relevant knowledge to improve the human condition. These skills represent the basic behavioral competencies which the social studies program must instill within youth during the remainder of the twentieth century. The successful attainment of these competencies will be dependent upon integrating both methodologies and research findings from the behavioral science disciplines into the teaching-learning strategies in secondary social studies at an increasing rate.

Critical Analysis. Teaching students the skills of critical thinking, or reflective inquiry, is vital to the promotion of independent thought.[3] Rarely is there one cause for, or one solution to, the many crucial problems besetting individuals or society. Developing the techniques of reflective inquiry improves the student's ability to view social issues in a relative rather than a purely descriptive context. The skills of critical analysis also enable students to seek alternatives, improve the decision-making process, examine conflicting forces, and develop the ability to question doctrinaire and authoritarian positions regarding the significant questions of our time. The effective utilization of critical analysis is dependent upon student awareness of the mode of inquiry in the behavioral sciences, which consists of the formulation of hypotheses or assumptions which may be accepted or rejected, and the use of valid evidence in the consideration of the proposed hypothesis or assumption.

Clarifying Values. There is considerable support for the assumption that one of the most serious diseases of our times is valuelessness.[4] The confusion regarding the identification of human values on an individual basis, referred to by different authors as "self-actualization," "self-realization," "psychological health," "creativity," and "productivity," appears to be a notable characteristic of students and adults alike. Encouraging students to examine and make choices regarding individual and group value systems is a vital objective of social studies instruction. The foremost problem in promoting valuing abilities on the part of students arises when the questions being considered are of a highly controversial nature. In many such instances, the social studies teacher is uncertain, or is fearful of influencing the traditional value orientation of a particular community. Nevertheless, teachers must make a conscientious effort to encourage students to examine the several sides of controversial public issues, social and cultural mores, and divergent individual and group behavioral patterns. Students should be urged to define their own value systems by analyzing their everyday reactions to other individuals and events regardless of how controversial. Once they achieve an awareness of the values they presently believe, students can gain some insight into the many alternatives open to them in today's complex society, in which the diversity of moral viewpoints and the range of availability for opportunities are extremely wide. Students should comprehend that through the examination of their reactions to actual situations, they can begin to understand their opinions with regard to particular issues confronting society. Most significantly, perhaps, students should be encouraged to become involved in the value conflicts that continually arise, since, thereby, they will have the opportunity to select the particular value alternative which is right for them as individuals. The primary responsibilities of the teacher are, first, to prepare students to make the most rational decisions possible about the particular value issue under discussion and, second, to prepare students to recognize what constitutes mere indoctrination or opinion concerning controversial national, international, and social issues and behavioral characteristics.

Decision-Making Strategies. The traditional social studies curriculum has failed to a considerable degree in the preparation of students to make either common day-to-day decisions or major decisions which might affect their future lives and the lives of others.[5] Instructional methodologies which stress the memorization and retention of factual knowledge must be broadened to the extent that theoretical and abstract subject content can be transferred from the social studies classroom and applied by students to the solution of the actual problems that continually confront all individuals. It is vital that the social studies program place much more emphasis upon teaching students the skills of decision-making, such as techniques for gathering evidence and the differences between positive and negative affirmation regarding such evidence, and help them to recognize the potential consequences and risks involved in making decisions in actual life situations.

Developing Self-Esteem. In spite of the disappointments and failures that individuals experience throughout their lives, most people manage to think sufficiently well of themselves to be encouraged to continue their vocational and personal goals.[6] However, there are many people who, after experiencing such disappointments, lose every vestige of self-esteem; they view themselves as failures in every respect; there is no more to do or to attempt. These people feel they have no "place" in the world, no worth, no significance, no ability, no judgment, and no future except more failure and guilt. Such a condition can easily develop into a serious depressive state. Youth of secondary school age are oftentimes uncertain or confused about their present lives and their futures, both personally and vocationally. Their self-image is, in many instances, largely shaped by adult attitudes toward them. As a consequence, youth may attempt to develop their lives and attitudes entirely around what they believe to be the hopes and aspirations which others, particularly parents and other adults, have for them. Dealing with such situations is not easy, but the social studies instructor should make students aware that all people possess a strong desire for self-esteem. Furthermore, teachers must encourage students to develop a feeling of independence with regard to their own personal and career interests and expectations, and must provide youth with the understanding that to feel alone in thoughts and ambitions can be, in many instances, a positive human quality.

The Shaping of Personality. From the instant of birth, every human possesses an individuality and, thus, a unique personality.[7] To what extent do humans inherit their personality from their parents? To what extent does one's social environment influence the development of his or her behavioral characteristics? What combination of factors influence youth to emerge as scientists or grocers, Republicans or Democrats, successes or failures? What determines moral values, sexual attitudes, degree of dependence on family and friends? Why does one feel inferior to some and superior to others? In essence, what combination of factors molds the individual personality? By the time students are of secondary school age, they are experiencing psychological and physical changes that tend to alter the relatively static personality pattern that characterized them during their elementary school years. Many youth examine themselves inwardly in an attempt to restructure their personality traits. A major responsibility of the social studies curriculum is to provide students with an opportunity to analyze the dual factors of heredity and environment, and the numerous other forces which influence and mold the human personality. In addition, students should become acquainted with the instinctual element of human personality, known as the "id," and with the sense of individuality, termed the "ego." Furthermore, it is the responsibility of social education to make students aware that adolescence is a period of conflicting demands between parents, society, and individual needs. In addition, this is the time in their lives when students should become acquainted with potential personality and emotional problems, as well as with the modern social attitude toward such problems and with the types of psychotherapeutic techniques utilized to solve them.

Improving Human Relationships.   Whether on the international, national, family, peer group, or individual levels, perhaps the most crucial problem confronting mankind today involves the improvement of human relations.[8] For many youth of secondary school age who are self-conscious about their identity and future goals, human relationships is an area of particular concern. In many instances, the desire to be accepted by a peer group results in conformity and blind role-playing at the expense of one's own individuality and freedom for emotional development and change. The social studies curriculum has the responsibility for instilling within students an awareness of some of the limitations of role-playing, such as how roles oftentimes prevent people from establishing friendships and knowing one another. Furthermore, it must be emphasized to students that learning to accept one's limitations, while at the same time maintaining a positive self-image, is vital to understanding the problems confronting others. All individuals desire genuine friendships with other people. Many times, however, they are held back by the fear of being known as they really are, or by an inability to accept others who do not measure up to their expectations. The social studies instructor must strive to make students aware that no one is perfect, that all people make mistakes, and that it is essential to continue to care for people regardless of their apparent imperfections.

Social Participation.   Active participation in the nation's social, political, and economic institutions by all segments of society is absolutely vital to the preservation of our democratic ideals.[9] Students must achieve the awareness that it is the responsibility of all citizens to actively engage in bringing about social and political change, changes which will continue to become necessary as a result of the nation's rapid technological and cultural advancement. A dynamic and expanding democratic society cannot afford passive obedience to local, state, or federal authority.

Organized Knowledge. The attainment of knowledge about social, political, and economic realities will continue to be an important goal of social education.[10] However, instead of imparting knowledge for knowledge's sake, teachers must enable students to achieve the intellectual competencies necessary to determine and select the subject matter that is relevant to the consideration and solution of personal problems and social issues. Thus, the appropriate knowledge comprising the social studies curriculum will depend upon the practical needs of the individual and of society, rather than upon the sophisticated structure of the academic disciplines. The purpose of knowledge in secondary education will be to provide ideas and concepts that can be used by students to promote critical thought, values analysis, and active social participation so that they can become productive, rational, and humane members of society.

COMPETENCY/PERFORMANCE-BASED TEACHER EDUCATION

In addition to the national curricular trend in social studies education to develop behavioral competencies for youth, a closely related movement, which will significantly affect future procedures for the preparation and certification of social studies teachers, as well as teachers in all curricular areas, is currently gaining nationwide momentum. In an attempt to improve the effectiveness of classroom instruction, leading social studies educators in all states are devoting a considerable amount of time, energy, and financial resources to the identification of competencies for social studies teachers based upon actual performance in instruction, rather than solely upon credit hours in the particular subjects being taught. Again, the emphasis is upon the identification of the particular classroom behaviors that should be demonstrated by the successful social studies teacher.

The national movement to shift teacher education to a performance or competency base, and to make demonstrated teaching competence the criterion for certification, began in 1970. Specifically, the basic performance- or competency-based model consists of three logically sequential steps. The first is to "stipulate" (identify and develop), in behavioral terms, the particular "competencies" (behaviors, skills, abilities) of the successful teacher. The second step is to develop "measures" (evaluation devices) to determine the degree to which the teacher possesses these competencies. Third is to design a teacher education program which demonstrably "produces" these competencies in the individual teacher.[11]

Competency/performance-based programs of teacher education probably will not be refined and finalized in all fifty states before the end of the present decade.

This innovation in teacher preparation and certification has been referred to as "the most significant lever for educational reform since Sputnik,"[12] and as "one of the most influential and important developments in this progressive effort to advance the process of schooling."[13] Furthermore, as this national movement gains momentum, instructional competencies for social studies teachers have already been identified and compiled by several states.[14] An examination of these competencies provides increasingly substantial evidence that both the performance criteria, or specific behaviors, for teachers, and the desired learning-objectives outcomes for students, are heavily weighted toward the methodology and subject content of the behavioral sciences, since the central theme of the performance-based models is upon improving the interrelationships and interaction among individuals, groups, and society through classroom instruction.

CONTENT RELEVANCY IN SOCIAL EDUCATION

The social studies curriculum provides for instruction in both the domestic and international realms. The emphasis of this discussion is on the national dimension of social education.

Throughout the evolution of the social studies curriculum in the United States, one of the constant tasks confronting educators has involved the problem of selecting those subject-matter topics which will most adequately meet the immediate and future needs of each generation of students. During these last decades of the twentieth century, American society is beset by many pressing social issues that need resolution. The nation's primary resource for resolving these problems is the human resource. It would seem vital, therefore, that society's problems be reflected in the content emphasis of the social studies program, so that this generation of students might be better equipped to understand, confront, and contribute toward their solution.

Enumerated below are some of the crucial social issues that our nation is already experiencing. This series of problems will confront American society until the year 2000 and probably well into the twenty-first century.

1. Futuristics	11. Highway stress
2. Birth control and family planning	12. Murder
3. Genetic manipulation	13. Suicide
4. Euthanasia	14. Boredom, both from leisure and age
5. Environmental pollution	15. Sex
6. Nourishment	16. Divorce
7. Psychological trauma	17. Juvenile delinquency
8. Alcohol	18. Prison reform
9. Drug abuse	19. Mental deficiency
10. Venereal disease	20. Neurosis and psychosis

Each of these problems involves either individual or group behavioral patterns. Therefore, if the social studies curriculum is to prepare youth to strive toward the successful resolution of these human issues, it must stress relevant knowledge and must draw increasingly upon content materials from the behavioral sciences —the disciplines that deal directly with these crucial problems. Throughout Chapters 4, 5, and 6, an attempt is made to develop effective instructional strategies that will facilitate the teaching of several of these significant behavioral science themes in the secondary social studies.

At the conclusion of each of the major themes discussed in Chapters, 4, 5, and 6, there follow some suggested "Assumptions for Student Inquiry." These have been developed to aid social studies teachers in motivating reflective inquiry in their classroom discussion of these topics. Each assumption is designed to promote critical analysis on the part of the individual student. A negative but recurring criticism of contemporary social studies instruction is that the subject content is descriptive rather than interpretive, resulting in instructional techniques which encourage the accumulation of absolute facts rather than relative concepts. The paradox of this situation is obvious when one of the main behavioral objectives of social studies instruction has been to promote the skills of critical inquiry and independent thinking in relative context.

The effective utilization of the inquiry method in social education is based upon the formulation of hypotheses or assumptions concerning aspects of the human condition. Through examining and questioning the assumptions, students should be motivated to gather data and evidence in order to support or reject each of the assumptions rather than accepting it as a valid statement. Through such a strategy, it is hoped, the students will achieve greater abilities in critical analysis and interpretive thought patterns, which they might later apply to the many and highly complex social issues that will confront them throughout their lifetimes. For classroom purposes, each theme and the accompanying assumptions might be reproduced and presented to each member of the class as a means of motivating spontaneous reflection and discussion. Optimistically, it is hoped that these examples of the inquiry technique could be applied to each significant issue considered in the social studies program.

CHAPTER 4

Futuristic Studies in Social Education

POSTTECHNOLOGICAL SOCIETY AND THE HUMAN CONDITION

Throughout the history of mankind, predictions of future events have found receptive audiences: during the thirteenth century, the English scientist Roger Bacon discussed the development of such things as optical instruments and motor boats; in the fifteenth century, Leonardo da Vinci wrote about tanks and helicopters; in the nineteenth century, Jules Verne described trips to the moon. Man has always been interested in where he is going. Since humanity's continued existence is dependent upon its making intelligent decisions about the future, such fascination has taken on a very practical dimension. Along with the changes in social mores and attitudes, greater numbers of people are demanding a role in planning the future. The social studies curriculum must provide students with an understanding of how significant future challenges will be with regard to our national survival, social problems, religion, marriage and family life, and in our political processes.

It is vital that social studies teachers immerse themselves in the new field of futuristics—the study of future prospects and possibilities affecting the human condition. Futuristics, as an academic area, is already being taught at many major universities for the purpose of encouraging students to achieve an awareness that they can contribute to the development of a much better national and global society than they ever dreamed of. The perspective of futurism is very important for today's students, since they know they can do nothing about the past.[1]

In technologically advanced societies, the sociologist Max Kaplan once observed, the masses toiled so that the elite could play. In posttechnological society, he predicted, the elite will toil so that the masses can play. The day will come, Kaplan predicted, when a man will go to the bank and borrow $10,000—and 5,000 hours. The uses he makes of those future hours may be defined by the goals evolved for "creative" retirement today. Another contemporary, historian Arnold Toynbee, believes that the future of civilization will depend on how we use our increased leisure time, while Marshall McLuhan notes that learning is already in the process of becoming both the dominant employer and the source of new wealth in our society. In addition, other demographers and sociologists predict that we must solve the problems involved in feeding a global population that is expected to double in forty years. For instance, it is pointed out that if population

26

increase is not checked, more than one-half of the world's population will live in huge, overcrowded urban areas by the year 2050.[2]

Currently, man possesses the skills and technological abilities to solve many of the societal and environmental problems that confront the human condition. For instance, computer and nuclear technologies, although relatively new and somewhat fearful, have unlimited potential for making planet earth more habitable than ever before. Mankind has a real opportunity to create a utopia. It is felt by many that mankind will create a utopia because goodwill and optimism will win over human selfishness and pessimism. The increasing global transnational organizations should eventually reduce the threats of both limited wars and thermonuclear holocaust for nationalistic motives. Likewise, the rivalries of intense nationalism should be modified during the future, resulting in greater international cooperation in the application of human knowledge and scientific technology to solve the pressing problems of population growth and famine, eradicating disease, increasing food production, promoting environmental control, and preventing natural-resource depletion.[3]

In the creation of this more positive world of tomorrow, social studies teachers will play a vital role, for they are responsible for equipping the nation's youth with an understanding of the global human condition. As a major instructional theme, social studies teachers should provide youth with a comprehension of the tremendous advancements that mankind has made, and of its potential for achievements in the future that will astound the imagination.

It would seem imperative, therefore, that social studies teachers place a priority upon gaining considerable insight into the new field of futurism. Since past human tragedies are irreversible, youth must be encouraged to achieve a futuristic perspective, since it is only during that future that today's student can have influence. As students give consideration to the many potential future developments, such as new types of family relationships, new forms of international relationships, new governmental, economic, and social systems, new types of leisure time and creative abilities, they should almost inevitably become involved in the type of future trends and events they wish to be realized. Equipped with this motivation, students may begin to accept responsibility for making them a reality for all of mankind.

To motivate student interest in futuristic studies, social studies instructors continually encourage students to ask questions concerning what they consider to be the future developments and innovations that will affect the daily lives of individuals and society, both domestic and international.[4] Regardless of the particular social studies course involved, many opportunities arise continually for the instructor to develop futuristic analysis around the following suggested topics which would be appropriate for junior and senior high school students:

1. Have students determine what they consider to be the major social problems confronting mankind and present their ideas about how to solve these problems, describing their own views of a utopian world in which they would like to live.

2. Ask students to visualize some of the new technological and scientific inventions and innovations which could drastically improve the way of life of individuals living both in technologically advanced societies and in less advanced societies.
3. Have students engage in research projects for the purpose of determining some of the innovations and changes in life-styles that professional futurists view as highly probable.
4. Introduce students to the *Futurist,* a periodical that concentrates on reporting the ideas and predictions that leaders from all walks of life are making for the future.
5. Ask each student to select a vocation or profession in which he is individually interested and present the changes in the specific vocation which may occur during the future.
6. Encourage students to prepare a list of vocations, careers, or professions which are presently very important to the welfare of the United States and the American people but may diminish substantially in significance by the year 2000.
7. Similarly, have students develop a list of careers or professions that are either very new or nonexistent today but may become very significant to the national interest during the remaining decades of the present century and well into the twenty-first century.
8. Have students enumerate what they consider to be the most serious social, economic, and political problems that will confront the United States and other nations during the remainder of the present century and throughout the twenty-first century.

The following selected hypotheses or assumptions are designed to promote reflective inquiry of several futuristic trends. An instructional strategy would be to divide the social studies class into an appropriate number of subgroups and assign each group one of the assumptions. Individual group members would then be responsible for stating hypotheses, undertaking independent research, formulating generalizations, and either accepting or rejecting the assumption on the basis of the data collected.

Assumptions for Student Inquiry

1. Due to the continued advancements in technology and automation, human skill and ability will become significantly less important to maintain high standards of living in technologically advanced societies such as the United States, resulting in retirement ages dropping from sixty-five to seventy to ages forty to forty-five by the year 2000.
2. By the year 2000, progress in science and medical technology will increase life expectancy from the current male-female average of seventy-two years to an average of ninety to ninety-five or even one hundred years.
3. As a result of continued technological advancements, a two- or three-day work-week will replace the five- or five-and-one-half-day work-week in most vocations and professions within the foreseeable future.
4. An individual's work or profession will become less and less the main goal in his or her life. Once the source of fulfillment and self-esteem, a career or profession will become less significant in the achievement of these roles.
5. A greater proportion of the population will consider leisure time as an opportunity for the "fuller" and more satisfying life.

6. New means of leisure time will be developed. Although the work ethic will change, people in technologically advanced nations, such as the United States, will continue to possess a strong desire to be creative and productive in their use of leisure time.
7. Time will become the greatest national resource of the United States. How it is used will provide a model for the remainder of the world's nations.
8. American attitudes toward such status symbols as ownership will be greatly modified. Thus, the rental business from homes to automobiles will become common.
9. The nation's educational system is producing too many educated people to be adequately absorbed into the economy in the near future. Thus, receiving federal welfare will be common for most of the population in order to maintain our high living standard.
10. In the future, the majority of the population in technologically advanced societies will spend most of their adult lives going to school or pursuing education as a career rather than working in vocations and professions.
11. By the end of the 1970s, private automobiles will be banned from many urban centers and replaced by public transportation systems.
12. Public schools "without walls" will become the rule; entire metropolitan areas will serve as the classroom, and as curricula become more socially relevant, students will learn to deal with problems and people by experiencing them.

Contrary to much of the social negativism that students watch, hear, and read via the mass media, the American educational system, and primarily the social studies program, must afford significantly greater opportunities for students to be aware of the positive aspects of mankind, both nationally and internationally, and the future prospects for nearly unlimited social betterment in global context.

NATIONAL POPULATION DYNAMICS

Ever since Thomas Malthus issued his classic warning about the danger of overpopulation in 1798,[5] scientists and laymen have argued the merits of his case. With the rapidly soaring population statistics of the twentieth century, the debate has continually increased in magnitude. Students hear the ideas of leading scientists with widely varying opinions, experts on population control, demographers, agricultural specialists, spokesmen of Western nations, Communist nations, and Third World or less-advanced nations. There are also reports from ecologists, politicians, government agencies, commissions, and other sources with divergent viewpoints.

It continues to be a rather negative reflection upon the American educational system that no nationwide curricular reform movement is advancing population education as one of its major goals. There currently are no major interdisciplinary or multidisciplinary social studies programs, from either the social sciences or the behavioral sciences, that directly treat the study of national or international population issues.

Throughout the arguments concerning population increase and the social, economic, and political ramifications of overpopulation, a debate which will continue well into the future, it would appear that the only truly effective instructional strategy which the social studies instructor can employ at the secondary level is to be certain that students are presented with all sides of this complex and emotional social issue. In addition, it would seem imperative that in the discussion of controversial subjects, such as overpopulation, students should be encouraged to utilize the inquiry method so that they might formulate hypotheses concerning this topic and, thereby, reflect upon this crucial issue in a relative rather than purely absolute context throughout their lifetime.

POPULATION INCREASE IN THE UNITED STATES

In futuristic perspective, the adequacy of a nation's technological and agricultural resource base is comparable to peace or thermonuclear holocaust as a crucial issue. It has direct implications for both the optimum size of the population and the standard of living which that population might enjoy. However, only recently have Americans been confronted with the premise that millions of inhabitants of the United States may be on the verge of starvation within the foreseeable future, that the nation's global position of power and prestige may plunge drastically as a result of overconsumption of nonreservable resources, that a substantial drop in the material standard of living is inevitable unless that natural rate of population increase is significantly curbed, and even extreme positions, such as that city dwellers will die from a lack of oxygen and water in our major urban areas unless drastic action is taken to significantly reduce air and water pollution. These and countless other issues are involved in the debate over the ability of our natural environment to support a continued increase in humanity. Again, the problems and prospects related to this contemporary issue are directly within the domain of the social studies curriculum.

Current Demographic Characteristics and Projections

With a current population of approximately 213 million people, and some predictions projecting an increase to a total of between 265 and 300 million by the end of the present century,[6] there is a great deal of support among several influential segments of American society today for the belief that the United States is in danger of becoming seriously overpopulated in the near future. In direct reference to this phenomenal increase, one national expert on the relationship between man and his environment has stated that "each American has roughly 50 times the negative impact on the earth's life-support systems as the average citizen of India. . . . Clearly population growth among Americans is much more serious than population growth in underdeveloped countries."[7] Such a view is exemplary of the emotional nature of the population increase-resource availability debate in the United States at the present time.

The weight of evidence, as presented through the mass media and such organizations as the Population Reference Bureau and the Planned Parenthood-World Population Federation, supports the premise that the United States is in immediate danger of becoming seriously overpopulated in relation to the energy and resource capabilities necessary to maintaining its global power position and extremely high living standard. Indeed, large-scale famine has been predicted! The answer to this national problem, according to these groups, is to drastically curb population increase immediately by reducing the natural rate of population increase.

As with all controversial social issues, however, there is another viewpoint, which students must be encouraged to examine, suggesting that such a bleak situation does not and will not exist during the foreseeable future. Contrary to those who predict a national population explosion, with tragic social, economic, and political consequences, unless the natural rate of population increase is stabilized, the latter philosophy makes no such dire predictions and foresees no need to reduce population increase in the United States. For this reason, it is the primary responsibility of the social studies instructor to give adequate consideration to both divergent schools of thought.

Overpopulation and Doomsday

Even though the United States has only about 6 percent of the world's total population, the nation consumes about 40 percent of the world's production of raw materials (not including food).[8] This privileged resource position cannot continue if the global economic gap is ever to be narrowed significantly, according to those who consider the United States to be overpopulated presently and tragically so in the immediate future if demographic trends are not reversed. This group supports the thesis that the nations which are the most populated are the nations whose people, by virtue of their numbers and activities, are most rapidly depleting their environmental capabilities to support human life. With its large population, extremely high living standard, and continued technological growth, the United States is, according to this view, the most overpopulated nation on earth because it cannot sustain its present level of national development if the current rate of population increase is not substantially curbed.

In a comparison with the Republic of India, when considering the ability of our natural environment to continually support high standards of living, the view is expressed that in Indian equivalents of resource use, the population of the United States is at least 4 billion! Furthermore, the rate of population increase is more alarming. This premise is supported by pointing out that our rate of population increase of slightly over 1.5 percent per year is ten times as serious as the Indian growth rate of 2.5 percent per year since the American citizen consumes so much more of the nation's resources to maintain his affluent materialistic standards. Indeed, if our numbers continue to rise, our standard of living will drop so drastically that by the year 2000 any surviving Americans might consider today's average Asian to be well off.[9]

Continuing, this group hypothesizes that our economic system is based upon the concept of continued growth in population and productivity, since this strategy was successful when the United States was an underpopulated nation with excess resources. Yet neither resources, the economy, nor anything else can expand indefinitely in the future. Using one vital resource as an example, it is noted that the United States currently depends upon petroleum for 78 percent of its energy resources. While constituting a mere 6 percent of the world's population, the nation consumes more than one-third of the earth's energy. Equally alarming is that so much of this one-third is wasted energy in a relative sense—since it is utilized to maintain a highly "sophisticated" quality of life. A civilization, they maintain, is comparable to a living organism. Its longevity is a function of its metabolism. The higher the metabolism (the standard of living) the shorter the life, and the United States has now run its course and is confronted with a tragedy even greater and more imminent than that facing the less-developed nations.[10]

What can be done to slow the rate of resource environmental destruction in the United States? Those who fear a serious overpopulation problem in the near future offer one basic approach. The nation must reverse the rate of population growth, since the nation has many more people now than it can continue to support at anything near today's level of affluence. The nation must achieve what is referred to as zero population growth[11] as rapidly as possible if we are to continue to survive as a technologically advanced nation with a continued increase in living standards.

Is There Really a Population Problem?

The relativity involved in support of an overpopulation problem in the United States, however, must be introduced by social studies teachers. In Mathusian terms, the claim that the United States will have a serious population problem during the near future is difficult to support. For instance, it must be pointed out to students that even though the population of the United States continues to increase, the birth rate during 1974 was lower than at any time during the nation's history. As a result, the nation is moving toward the much debated state of zero population growth—the theoretical point at which births balance deaths. Furthermore, our population is not pressing upon the domestic food supply, nor is there substantial evidence that it will during the next decades. There is no indication that the United States is threatened by what Malthus referred to as the "positive checks" on population growth of famine or pestilence, and the third positive check—war—which, for the United States, is entirely independent of internal population dynamics. Instead, the thesis of overpopulation in the United States is closely related to the quality and safety of our natural environment and social surroundings. The primary question for student discussion, therefore, is whether our natural and cultural environments are significantly threatened by the nation's natural rate of population increase.

Due to the controversial nature of the population-resource utilization issue, social studies teachers must present the viewpoint (although a minority view) of those who do not believe that the United States will be confronted with an overpopulation problem or that substantially reducing population growth will reduce resource depletion and environmental pollution. Indeed, those expressing this philosophy do not feel that our natural environment or energy-resource base is in danger of being destructively exploited to the point of not being capable of supporting continued technological growth and individual affluence.

Students should understand that the basic assumption expounded by the opponents of population control in the United States encourages the increased expenditure of capital to alter or continually reconstruct the natural environment and its resources, thus improving the environment's ability to support greater numbers and densities of people. In addition, this group strongly encourages a reordering of the nation's fiscal-appropriation priorities and the placing of more emphasis upon improving the human, economic, and social conditions of the nation's citizens.[12] In their view, giving more attention to the development of the natural environment, natural resources, and the social environment, rather than reducing and controlling the natural rate of population increase, is the answer to the population question in the United States for future years.

In essence, this view holds that the United States, with a current population of 213 million and a projected increase to 265–300 million by the beginning of the twenty-first century, will experience absolutely no environmental or social crises. This thesis is based upon the highly sophisticated technological capability and the enormous amount of investment capital that the nation possesses. Therefore, the opponents of population control firmly believe that an expanding economy is absolutely dependent upon a steadily increasing population, and that if the nation's investment capital is directed toward constantly improving the human condition and developing the environmental resource potential in the United States, a population problem based upon absolute number of people will not become a negative social issue during the future.

Zero Population Growth and Demographic Trends

Closely related to the overpopulation-environmental depletion debate in the United States is the concept of zero population growth, which for some time has received a great deal of support from several national agencies committed to reducing the natural rate of population increase. Their national goal is to achieve zero population growth as soon as possible. Specifically, zero population growth equals a two-child family, since under current conditions of infant mortality in the United States, an average of 2.1 children per female would, in a few decades, result in a stable population for the nation.

By late 1974, the United States birth rate had suddenly fallen lower than many experts had predicted. For the first time, the birth rate had fallen below the 2.11 babies for each couple regarded as necessary for the population to replace itself.

In 1972 there were 2.025 babies per couple. In 1973, unofficial tabulations revealed that there were only 1.9 babies per couple, a record low.[13]

Many demographic experts predict that if this trend continues, the United States will have achieved zero population growth—where birth rates and death rates are the same and the population remains approximately the same size year after year—in another fifty years, or by 2025.[14] Demographers note that if the birth rate remains steady for the next half-century at two children per couple, today's population of 212 million would expand by only about 25 percent to approximately 265 million. But if the birth rate should go up to an average of three children per couple, the population would mushroom by about 85 percent to 392 million.

As noted previously, the primary argument for achieving zero population growth involves the major theory that the only viable approach to the population problem in the United States is to be found in encouraging Americans to moderate their long-standing attitudes toward large families. Rather than idealizing large families, small (two-children) families should become the ideal. Furthermore, instead of promoting forms of economic growth which will increasingly deplete and pollute our natural environment, we must insist that we clean up as we go no matter what the cost. Instead of measuring our material welfare by the amount of our consumption, the populace must become deeply concerned about enhancing the quality of life in its various forms.

In a more practical sense, however, it must be noted that perhaps the most pervasive element in the decreasing birth rate is not the theoretical debates among demographers but, rather, the changing role of women in American society. Presently 43 percent of all women have jobs outside the home.[15] Experts expect that this percentage will steadily increase. In addition, improvement and availability of contraceptives, liberalized abortion laws, and the soaring cost of rearing children have resulted in the situation that more women are choosing to have fewer children or none at all. In addition, it must be pointed out that behavioral scientists and demographers are divided on the issue of whether zero population growth, once achieved, will have positive or negative results for the nation. Some maintain that a free economy requires constant expansion, and fear that an end to population growth will produce social and economic stagnation. But, on the other hand, many experts agree that the United States would be better off if its rate of economic expansion could be considerably reduced. Each of these viewpoints provides social studies teachers with many opportunities to design hypothetical questions for students regarding future population trends and their implications for the continued development of the United States. In any event, students must be made aware that long before zero population growth is achieved, which some demographers predict will happen around 2025, when they expect the population to be approximately 300 million, the United States will be a considerably different nation than it is today in many social and economic respects, necessitating the development of new behavior patterns for a large proportion of the American population.

Assumptions for Student Inquiry

1. The United States, with a current population of 212 million and a projected increase totaling approximately 300 million by the end of the present century, must be considered overpopulated.
2. The major reason that the United States is considered to be overpopulated is the rapid depletion of the nation's natural-resource base.
3. The United States cannot be considered overpopulated since the technological and scientific capacity possessed by the nation has the capability to continually create new resources from the natural environment to adequately support an increasing population without any sacrifice in the living standard.
4. The United States would not be overpopulated if capital expenditure was directed toward altering the natural environment, thus improving its ability to support greater densities of population.
5. The United States would not be considered overpopulated if the nation's fiscal spending priorities placed more emphasis upon improving the human, economic, and social condition of many of the nation's citizens.
6. Giving more attention to both the natural and human environments and the nation's resource base, rather than reducing and controlling the natural rate of population increase, is the answer to the population problem.
7. The United States must achieve zero population growth as rapidly as possible in order to reduce the depletion of our natural resources, control environmental pollution, and maintain our high material standard of living.
8. There appears to be only one viable approach to the population problem in the United States. This is the long tedious route of encouraging Americans to moderate their basic attitudes toward large families. Rather than idealizing large families and creating them, small (two-children) families should become the ideal.
9. Population or birth control is not the business of the federal government, private agencies and groups, or organized religion.
10. The larger the nation's population, the greater will be its economic and social development and, thus, the higher the standard of living for the entire population.

GLOBAL RESOURCES, ENVIRONMENTAL CONTROL, AND THE ECOSYSTEM

The purpose of the following discussion is to portray the interrelationships between ecology and human behavior patterns in global context. The writer has attempted to provide teachers with instructional strategies designed to improve the teaching of the concept of the interconnectivity between the earth's natural resource base, environmental limitations, international technological development, and continued population growth.

As a direct result of the constant national and international attention given to social problems associated with the energy crisis, environmental pollution, and overpopulation, all social studies teachers will continue to be confronted with the following basic question: How many people is the earth, or a particular global region, capable of supporting if there is to be a reduction in such undesired social conditions as poverty, famine, malnutrition, riots, war, and destructive exploitation of the environment? Indeed, there is little doubt that these concerns will continue to gain significance for social studies instruction during future years.

POPULATION AND RESOURCE UTILIZATION IN WORLD PERSPECTIVE

Global Demographic Data

According to the *United Nations Demographic Yearbook,* the world's population increased by 76 million people in one year to 3.8 billion.[16] Presently (1975), however, this figure is slightly outdated, and there are over 3.9 or nearly 4 billion people on earth. More than half, 2.254 billion, live in Asia. Europe is a distant second with 470 million people. The People's Republic of China is the world's most populous nation with over 800 million, followed by the Republic of India with approximately 575 million.[17]

On an annual basis, the latest data indicate, approximately 133 million births occur and 55 million people die, leaving nearly 78 million human beings added to the world's population each year. For secondary students, the significance of the current total world population and the yearly increase becomes more meaningful when the figures are placed on a time continuum which reveals that the global rate of population growth has been increasing for over two thousand years. It should be pointed out that it took about ten thousand years for the world's population to grow from 5 million to 500 million in 1650; thus, population was doubling approximately every thousand to fifteen hundred years. World population reached 1 billion in 1850; the doubling time had been reduced to two hundred years. A world population of 2 billion was reached by 1930, which represents a doubling in eighty years. It has taken only forty-five years, to 1975, to double world population again, and the projections indicate that global population will double again in the next twenty-five years, or by the year 2000. Thus, at the present rate of increase, the world population would reach 100 billion in less than two hundred years (compared with 4 billion today)—and more than 3,000 billion in less than five hundred years. In about fifteen hundred years, unless there are migrations to other planets, the weight of humanity will exceed the weight of the planet earth. Another way of presenting this situation to students would be to point out that if current growth rates continue, in nine hundred years there would be about one hundred people per square yard on the earth's surface.[18]

In global perspective, the world's people are divided into two major demographic groups: (1) The technologically advanced nations, comprising the United

States, Canada, Western Europe, the Soviet Union, Australia, New Zealand, and Japan. These modern societies have low birth rates (from seventeen to twenty-five per thousand) in approximate balance with existing death rates (eight to twelve per thousand). Consequently they have a slow rate of population growth. (2) The developing nations of Asia, Latin America, and Africa have a combined population of approximately 3 billion—nearly three-fourths of the people on earth! These regions have continuing high rates of population growth, ranging from thirty-nine to over fifty per thousand in population, and with declining death rates that range from ten to over thirty per two thousand in some African countries. One basic concept for student awareness is that the rate of population increase is still rising significantly in these regions of economic scarcity, while the urbanized-industrialized regions are gaining control of their population growth. For example, the United Nations recently estimated that more than 85 percent of the world's population growth for the remainder of this century, and throughout the twenty-first century, will be experienced in the less-developed societies of Asia, Africa, and Latin America.[19] A second important concept for student understanding is that the reduced rate of population growth in technologically advanced nations is due to what is referred to as the "demographic transition"— the transition from a high-birth-rate, high-death-rate culture (with low living standards) to a low-birth-rate, low-death-rate culture (with higher living standards). This transition began for the advanced nations in the mid-nineteenth century, while it has yet to begin in the two-thirds of the world's nations considered to be technologically less developed. Third, students should understand that in less-developed nations, children are highly valued. Not only do they play an important economic role, helping with farming or other jobs, but by supporting their parents in their old age, children also represent a form of social security. Just as important, children are also desired for themselves. A basic dictum is that parents will not stop having children until they believe that those they already have are going to survive. Furthermore, as long as demographers attempt to solve the population problem by emphasizing birth control exclusively, success in limiting population growth will prove elusive. Integrated programs of nutrition, sanitation, and public health services must be incorporated into a nation's overall program for family planning.

Population Increase and Resource Availability

During future decades, the social studies curriculum will be increasingly responsible for attempting to provide students with more adequate insights regarding the following basic social issues in relation to global demographic trends: Is the rate of population increase a source of national and international health, or is it a disease which must be eradicated? Are the extensive birth-control measures and family-planning programs that are being strongly encouraged in the less-advanced regions, which contain over two-thirds of the world's population, designed to help underdeveloped societies, or, as has been suggested, are these plans a racist plot to maintain the supremacy of the white race? Are the world's resources about to be depleted, or are there virtually limitless possibilities for resource expansion? Are the population projections expounded by doomsday demographers substantiated by evidence, or do such statistics represent a non-valid deception?

Availability of Energy Resources

It appears obvious that the populations of all biological species are limited by their environmental capabilities, and mankind is no exception. This planet has been appropriately termed "Spaceship Earth." It possesses a closed system as far as usable materials, or resources, are concerned. Furthermore, regardless of continued space exploration, there is currently no scientific evidence to support the belief that the earth's inhabitants can exploit and import resources from other planets in the solar system for use on earth. Earth is our natural habitat and probably will be for as long as the human species survives. Thus, its resource potentialities in terms of its population increase must continually be considered and reevaluated.

Students should achieve the realization that the demand for energy resources among the world's nations will more then double, some say triple, in a single decade, or by 1985.[20] The sources for all this energy for the next twenty-five years, however, are reasonably predictable. Today, out of current global energy consumption, 90 percent comes from fossil fuels—petroleum, gas, coal—and only 10 percent results from other sources combined (hydroelectricity, nuclear energy, and wood). By 1985 fossil fuels will almost certainly continue to provide three-quarters of the world's energy and by the year 2000 about the same proportion.[21]

By the end of the present century, the significance of coal as an energy resource will drop considerably (although production will increase enormously), and nuclear energy will account for about 20 percent of global energy needs. Indeed, during the decade of the 1970s, the world will consume more petroleum than all of the petroleum used by man since the dawn of history. From this substantiated evidence, students should achieve the realization that the world's energy resources will probably come mainly from fossil fuels for at least the next two generations. In answer to the basic question of whether there are enough fossil fuel sources available on a global basis to sustain these enormous demand increases in the future, the answer is probably yes.[22]

Future Energy Requirements

It must be emphasized to students, nevertheless, that the present dependence of the world's major technological societies, such as the United States, Northwestern Europe, the Soviet Union, and Japan, on energy resources from fossil fuels cannot go on indefinitely throughout the twenty-first century. There are limited amounts of such fuels on earth, laid down once and once only over a span of millions of years, and the technologically advanced nations are presently engaged in utilizing them during a relatively short span of human history. It would appear from national and international publications that the advanced nations have based their ability to maintain their high living standards and global power positions in the future on the strategy of supplying the necessary energy requirements upon the use of nonrenewable resources—energy resources that simply will not last. For instance, the best estimates available indicate that the petroleum on Alaska's North Slope may provide the United States with only a three- to five-year supply.[23] As a result, we have extended the nation's petroleum resources from something like twenty to twenty-five years! For that, we may have permanently damaged the ecosystem of Alaska. If the populations of technologically advanced nations are to maintain their living standards, it is highly probable that new sources of energy must be discovered. At this moment, the only new resource visible on a sufficient scale is nuclear energy. More importantly, however, most experts do not foresee the possibility of substantial nuclear (fission) power before the year 2000. Nuclear power, therefore, is the energy resource of the next century, while during this century's remaining two and one-half decades, man's energy requirements will continue to expand. Students should understand that the real energy crisis in future perspective lies in the need of the world's technological societies to develop indefinitely lasting, ecologically sound sources of energy for future development.

The Natural Environment and the Human Ecosystem

Regardless of individual views concerning what has also come to be known as the environmental crisis, it should be emphasized to students that even if some phenomena affect the ecological system only in one area, the entire system is affected. In other words, students should be encouraged to view the entire world, the natural environment, and its population as a single interlocking system, or ecosystem. It is impossible to do something someplace that has no direct or indirect environmental effect somewhere else. One of the major responsibilities of the social studies instructor is to instill a comprehension among students of the significance of the interconnections among population, pollution, environmental deterioration, war, and resource depletion. Environmental pollution, in its broadest sense, results from the fact that all forms of life by their very nature must, in order to survive, live off their environment—and, thereby, in some ways change it. Man, of course—especially industrialized man—is the greatest of all consumers of the materials in his environment, and is, therefore, the greatest of all producers of waste products.

During the early 1970s, public concern about environmental depletion and pollution reached an emotional peak. Many people became convinced that the natural environment was being rapidly exhausted, and that the populations in technologically advanced societies were about to choke to death from environmental pollution. This "crisis" was reflected by a plethora of educational publications, designed for both teacher and student consumption, which triggered panic on the one hand and overnight panaceas for environmental control on the other. Such emotional heights, however, cannot and should not be maintained, particularly when they influence the values and ideals of youth. Rather, what is needed is student awareness of the long-range interrelationships between the natural environment and the ever-increasing demands which will continue to be made upon it by mankind during future generations, as well as the alternatives which humanity possesses to preserve their environmental capabilities.

The Environment and Population: Interconnected Elements

In the human ecosystem, man assigns use or value to various elements of his environment and, therefore, refers to them as resources. Resources are not entirely of the natural environment or the cultural environment but, rather, are the result of interaction between the two environments. Regardless of future environmental issues of which students will be aware, they can place confidence in the theorem that the elements of the natural environment which mankind needs to serve as resources, and the nature and size of the resources necessary, depend upon not only the total population in a particular area but also upon human needs and desires as well as values and skills.

Mankind's resource requirements depend on the size, distribution, and social characteristics of a particular population. In global perspective, man is confronted with continued population growth, particularly in the less-developed regions, which will continue to demand and utilize a greater proportion of the earth's natural resources base in the future to increase their technology and raise living standards. In addition, the world's population will continue to urbanize and become concentrated in particular areas in all nations, such as urban, metropolitan, and megalopolitan nodes.[24] While each additional human being requires the basic human necessities, such as food, water, shelter, and space, he will also require more of these in the future. How much more man will derive from his environment depends upon his individual desires and his ability to satisfy them. On a global basis, mankind collectively is in the midst of a "revolution of rising expectations," involving a universal commitment to the concept of economic growth as an irreversible and irrepressible future need.

The availability of resources at any time in any area is the result of interrelationships between the natural environment, the size of man's requirements, and the means of developing the resources. One of the most basic societal elements involved in the interaction between man and the natural environment is the increasing technological sophistication that man will have at his disposal for discovering, producing, processing, and utilizing environmental resources. The range of technology available to various nations changes rapidly with time, education, and understanding. The continuous future growth and changing capability of mankind will contribute significantly to the dynamic issues involved in environmental resource utilization.

During future years, it will be the responsibility of the social studies program to point out that population patterns and concentrations attain greatest significance when the natural and cultural environments are considered in flexible terms. A most important principle is that a "resource" may be considered less a physical substance than a cultural or technological achievement. This applies not only to mineral resources, but also to water, soil, vegetation, and climate, as well as location. Although the natural habitat sets limits upon human activities and ambitions, man is capable of imposing his will upon the environment and creating resources. Resources, then, have reference only to man. But man is not constant, and human changes are accompanied by changes in what constitutes a resource and what man depends on.

The abilities and skills necessary for the development and utilization of the natural environment to supply the needs of man vary significantly on a global basis. As implied above, most of today's technologically less advanced societies are not economically underdeveloped because they do not possess natural resources. To the contrary, most of these nations are well endowed with a natural resource base but simply do not possess the education, the human abilities, or the capital to exploit and develop their resources. Thus, it is extremely difficult for these nations to become technologically developed and raise living standards for their people. On the other hand, many technologically advanced nations possess so much human skill and capital, and have developed their resources, economies, and living standards to such a scientific and sophisticated level, that they appear to be in danger of depleting their existing resource base and, as a result, their level of technological achievement and their standards of living.

Environmental Control vs. Environmental Pollution

There would appear to be increasing support among many experts for the rather terse but, perhaps, valid statement made recently by a world authority on environmental quality that "one of the sickest jokes of our age may be the so-called environmental and population crises."[25] It is further suggested that the intensity of the "crisis barrage," primarily from governmental agencies in the United States as well as other advanced nations, was designed to shift the concern of many people from more serious domestic and international problems. Again, regardless of the academics involved, environmental pollution and man's continued attempts to reduce it will continue to be a significant social and political issue for future decades.

In the laboratories and research facilities of many nations—but particularly the technologically advanced countries—scientists, social and behavioral scientists, and engineers of all varieties are at work on special problems raised by the ever-greater impact of humanity upon the natural environment. To understand the problems that will continue to absorb so much concern from scientists and environmentalists, as well as politicians representing the international community, and to better comprehend the contribution of a growing population to increased environmental pollution, students must distinguish two broad classes of pollutants.

The first class includes the major products of combustion associated with technological advancement—carbon monoxide, carbon dioxide, oxides of nitrogen, oxides of sulfur, and several measures of water pollution, including biochemical demand for oxygen and dissolved industrial solids.[26] The environmental pollutants in this group, once produced, endure in the environment for a relatively short time—short enough so that long-term accumulations are not a problem. These pollutants are easy to relate to future economic growth and population trends.

The second class of pollutants includes those which endure in the environment longer—radiation and pesticides, plus a wide and ever-changing variety of chemicals emitted by technological and scientific industries. Most such chemicals are highly poisonous. For many of these pollutants, future developments in environmental control will depend more upon improvements in technology than on reducing population and economic growth, since they are very difficult to relate directly to economic and population expansion.[27]

With regard to ecological and environmental problems, it must be understood that population growth is not the sole culprit in environmental damage. The real problem confronting the global ecological system is that increasing populations in all nations encourage the adoption of new and more intense technologies before the environmental side-effects are known. In essence, continued rapid population growth limits the options of nations, especially underdeveloped nations. In the case of the larger population, with less land per person and more people to accommodate, there are fewer alternatives, for environment is dependent upon advances in technology and changes in human life-styles. Slower population growth, on the other hand, offers nations the difference between various human-environmental choices and the necessity for abrupt and drastic action.

In summary, the ecological approach to environmental control views the natural world as a series of interrelated systems in a state of constant and dynamic change, into which the goals of mankind and of individual nations intrude as a variable or unbalancing factor. Thus, study and research dealing with multiple-choice and systems-analysis approaches to environmental problems must first place emphasis upon determining the changing behavior of mankind during future decades.

Environmental Control and Food Production

Civilization, as it is known today, could not have evolved, nor can it survive, without an adequate food supply. Nevertheless, it would seem that many of the world's leaders take the availability of food for granted, despite the fact that more than half of the world's population is hungry.[28] Similarly, the prophets of overpopulation continually reinterpret Malthusian doctrine and conclude that the only answer to the probability of global famine during the decade of the 1980s is to either reverse the natural rate of global population growth or increase food production three-fold by the end of the present century, so to maintain minimum dietary standards for the world's increasing population.[29]

Since the beginning of the nineteenth century, there have been two opposing philosophical views concerning population growth. These divergent theories have arisen from the adherents of Malthus, Marx, and Roman Catholicism. In 1798 the British social economist Thomas Malthus first formulated his general laws of population growth. His basic premise was that population tends to increase faster than the means of subsistence and, therefore, must be controlled, either by checking the rate of reproduction or by maintaining high death rates. Actually, he wrote that population, when unchecked, tends to increase in geometrical progression (1-2-4-8-16- etc.) every quarter-century, while "subsistence," or food production, increases only in arithmetical progression (1-2-3-4-5- etc.).[30] Sooner or later there must come a time when population greatly exceeds the supply of food and the other necessary commodities of life, and thus must be reduced by either "positive" or "preventive" checks. Until the mid-nineteenth century, widespread famine, disease, and war were the main "positive" checks that kept a population balanced with the means of subsistence. In addition, there were "preventive" or "prudential" checks, such as the postponement of marriage and continence, which resulted in a decline of the birth rate.

Expressing the opposite position concerning the demographic problems of emergent nations are the Communist ideologists, who remain fanatically opposed to the Malthusian principles and are scornful of any talk of population pressure on the means of food production, which they consider to be "cannibalistic." The contemporary Communist view is the result of the theories of Karl Marx (1818–1883), whose basic thesis was diametrically opposed to that of Malthus. According to the Marxist-Leninists, it was—and currently is—the antiquated social systems (namely, extreme forms of capitalism) under which two-thirds of the world's population live which cause low living standards, rather than the absolute population numbers or high rate of natural increase in the less-developed nations. For Marx, the overthrow of capitalism was a prerequisite to all social betterment, and the solution to the population problem would be automatic under socialist economic institutions.[31] Experience, however, has repudiated the sweeping views of both Malthus and Marx. Again, social studies teachers have the responsibility of introducing a moderate perspective on this serious but not insurmountable social problem.

Never before has it been possible to produce more food on an acre of land, yet never before have the victims of hunger been more numerous in the world. Every day some ten thousand people—most of them children—die in the developing nations as a result of illness caused by starvation and malnutrition.[32] Paradoxical as it may appear, the greatest extent of hunger is in the countries where the vast majority (65 to 90 percent) of the working population is engaged in agriculture. Only in the urbanized-industrialized nations are the people adequately nourished, although only 8 to 25 percent of the labor force are farmers. Between two-thirds and 70 percent of the world's people live in developing areas at little above bare subsistence levels, and over 50 percent of the world's population suffers perpetual hunger. Significantly, there is less food per capita in the world today than a year ago. The mandatory increase in food production for minimum development is calculated at 4 percent annually, yet the world has achieved an average of only 2 percent over the last decade, and even less in recent years.[33] Thus, today hungry nations; tomorrow starving nations.

During the contemporary period, widespread famine in the developing countries has been kept at bay by food imports, but supplies of food for this purpose are now near the vanishing point. Indeed, students should be aware that there are no surpluses of any major food commodities in the United States or anywhere else in the world. Furthermore, the panaceas of synthetic foods, synthesized proteins, hydroponics, desalinization of sea water, and food from the seas are all possibilities for the late 1980s, when the famines will already have arrived. The only valid answer, according to many, is to generate a marked and sustained increase in agricultural productivity in the developing countries themselves, and this assumes the application of an entirely new agricultural technology.

Most of the developing countries have the natural resources to double or treble their food production. However, this will require the input of every form of technical aid and research it is possible to utilize. But above all, the rural people of the world themselves must become involved, seeking to help themselves. For instance, in many advanced nations there is one adviser for approximately every seven hundred farmers; in many developing countries, on the other hand, there may be only one trained field worker for every twenty thousand or even thirty thousand cultivators,[34] a stark illustration of the enormous shortfall of this single resource, the human resource.

It should be emphasized, however, that the problem is not simply one of growing enough to feed the increasing population, for while global numbers increase, life-styles also change. In search for a better living standard more people migrate to the cities, yet the rural areas must still be able to feed them even as their own populations continue to expand. By 1975 urban populations in the developing countries will have increased to 26 percent of the whole, compared with 20 percent in 1970; by 1985 the figure is expected to increase to 31 percent.[35] The lesson is obvious. It is not enough for food production to keep abreast of the population expansion in these nations, it must increase far enough ahead to enable the entire economy to develop.

Can the Desert Bloom?

An examination of a world population map will disclose two highly significant facts: the arrangement of people on the earth is very uneven, and most of the earth's surface remains relatively uninhabited. A major generalization for student awareness is that the global pattern of population distribution reflects the opportunities for human groups to make a living. Presently, more than 75 percent of the world's 3.5 billion people is concentrated in three major clusters comprising approximately 20 percent of the earth's land area (Monsoon Asia, Western and Northwestern Europe, and Eastern North America), while nearly half of the earth's surface is inhabited by less than one person per square mile.

One of the foremost questions currently confronting mankind involves the potential capacity of the remaining 75-plus percent of the earth's land area, which remains largely uninhabited due to extreme environmental limitations, to support larger population densities. The chief deterrents to increasing food production, and thus the human "carrying capacity" in these marginal areas, are the high cost of constructing agricultural and technological facilities as well as the factor of cultural isolation. In addition, expanding cities utilize more and more territory, and usually the most potentially arable areas. An effective technique for motivating student inquiry concerning the world's environmentally negative regions involves a discussion of the Communist ideological view toward the natural environment. The Marxist believes that under Communism mankind will have available the necessary capital and technical ability to alter, reconstruct, or overcome the harsh nature of any marginal environment. Furthermore, the Communist ideologists claim that the Western philosophy is one of environmental determinism, which is used simply as an excuse to explain the abominable human condition existing in many of the world's developing areas.

With regard to the more than 75 percent of the earth's surface that is comprised of water, so far the oceans, seas, and major lakes have basically retained the nature of a hunting and gathering ground. Nevertheless, the potential of the oceans is infinite as a resource for food. With better knowledge of aquatic ecology, it should be possible to manipulate the oceans as commercial farmers do their environments, selecting the best habitat for each useful fish species, breeding better strains, and providing more plankton for feeding. But all of this must wait until the intensive oceanographic research now getting under way can lay a sound foundation for the agricultural development of the sea.

Population pressure and low living standards might be considered the most explosive forces in the modern world. Unless the problem of matching mankind and food production is solved, the world faces chaos in the form of not only hunger, poverty, and disease, but of bitterness, conflict, and violence of global proportions. During the past three centuries, world population has increased about fourfold. The growth over the past half-century has been nearly one billion. Obviously, this recent demographic expansion is unprecedented in human history. The current trend, long continued, is viewed by many as calamitous. Expressing the opposite thesis concerning global population dynamics are formidable religious organizations and political ideologists, who vigorously denounce the threat of a world demographic crisis. These latter groups, although representing a minority view, expound the assumption that outdated and backward social, economic, and political institutions, rather than absolute numbers of people, are responsible for the negative human condition which currently exists throughout much of the world.

Classroom discussions concerning population increase, environmental control, resource utilization, and food production should center around two sharply contrasting themes: one, of almost unrivaled dangers; the other, of new optimism that the problems associated with these social issues can be resolved during the remainder of this century. Furthermore, students must also be aware that the transition from emerging nation to advanced nation tends to be cyclic in many instances. The alleviation of social problems in one sector of the economy may result in the creation of equally serious difficulties in other areas. There is no universal blueprint for achieving well-balanced national growth. Individual societies are confronted with unique problems at varying stages of development. Development for many nations of the world is a long-term prospect and must be understood and appraised accordingly.

Assumptions for Student Inquiry

1. The current world population explosion is the most serious economic, social, or political problem confronting mankind today. It is even more significant than the continued possibility of thermonuclear war.
2. The rapid rate of population increase is not of world-shaking importance since a population distribution map would reveal that most of the earth's land surface, particularly in the developing areas, which are experiencing the most rapid increase, is very sparsely settled or uninhabited altogether.
3. The present rapid rate of population increase is not due to an increase in the birth rate but, rather, is mainly the result of medical technology and sanitation procedures which extend longevity and greatly reduce death rates.
4. An additional reason for Western concern about the great population increases in the non-Western world is based upon the racial issue. Since the vast majority of the world's expanding population is nonwhite, the white, or Caucasian, race, which predominates in Western Europe and North America, is rapidly becoming the world's smallest racial minority group.
5. The adoption by developing nations of a complete socialistic economic and political system, based upon the principle of central economic planning (i.e., Communism), would remove the problem of population pressure and low living standards, since the socialistic system would provide for a more equal distribution of the nation's resources and wealth than exists under the present quasi-capitalistic systems in these areas.
6. There is no such thing as an energy crisis or an environmental crisis. These two terms are simply scare phrases propagated by self-seeking politicians to remove people's thoughts from the more serious social issues confronting mankind.
7. Instead of a meager 4 billion people, the world's natural environment possesses the resource capability to support over 100 billion people if nations will spend the necessary capital to reconstruct the environment rather than only depleting it.
8. Increased population growth is the foremost cause of environmental pollution throughout the world today and will continue to be during the foreseeable future.

9. If thermonuclear war or worldwide famine does not drastically reduce population growth by the end of the century, environmental pollution will.

10. The resources of the earth's natural environment are limited, and at the present rate of consumption, the world's nations will deplete their resource base by the year 2050.

11. Continued global population growth increases the probability of both nuclear war and worldwide famine.

12. The Malthusian doctrine of population growth, expressed in 1798, is more valid today for two-thirds of the world's people than ever before, since, during the next fifteen to twenty years, world population will have increased to the point where mankind will destroy itself through famine, starvation, or wars for the control of food-producing areas.

13. If the wealth and technological abilities of mankind would be directed toward improving the productivity of the 70 to 75 percent of the earth's land surface which is presently considered environmentally marginal, or incapable of supporting large numbers of people, the problem of world overpopulation would cease to exist.

14. Western nations, as an excuse for not investing capital in marginal areas of the world to increase food production, use the concept of environmental determinism, or the impossibility of improving extreme environmental limitations, to explain why two-thirds of humanity exists on bare subsistence levels.

15. Contrary to Communist ideological pronouncements regarding environmental reconstruction, the Western capitalistic nations have done much more to increase the human "carrying capacity" of marginal areas of their countries than have the Communist nations.

16. Unless the potential of the earth's oceans and seas as a food-producing area is realized in the near future, there is little hope of adequately feeding the world's people by the year 2000.

17. It is immoral for governments, international or national organizations, religious groups, medical personnel, or health officials to influence the individual's reproductive capacity through encouraging the use of birth-control techniques, regardless of the economic, social, or political consequences which may be involved.

18. Although national and international organizations have given a great deal of attention to introducing birth-control programs in the developing nations during the last several years, very little progress has been made in convincing the masses of the desirability of various contraceptive techniques.

19. The greater the extent of urban growth in developing nations, the more acceptable birth-control techniques will become among the majority of the population in these areas.

20. Outdated religious beliefs and irrational political ideologies are the two primary reasons for the current population crisis which exists throughout two-thirds of the world today.

As a culminating activity to classroom discussions concerning contemporary global population dynamics, students should be provided the opportunity to examine the final "Plan of Action" report prepared by the United Nations World Population Conference, attended by representatives from 141 nations, which was held in Bucharest, Romania, during the late summer of 1974 for the purpose of promoting international participation in the activities of World Population Year, 1974.[36] Although this document represented a compromise in the continuous and bitter ideological debate between advanced, less-developed, and Communist nations over the priorities involved in population increase and resource availability, it adds clarity to several of the basic reasons why the world's nations have not as yet achieved full agreement in the controversial areas of population growth and environmental control. Furthermore, this conference also represented the broadest multigovernment agreement acceptable at this first attempt to arouse and focus coordinated international attention on the world's population problem.

CHAPTER 5

Personal Behavior Patterns

There would appear to be an increasingly greater diversity of individual behavior patterns, or personal life-styles, in the United States today than in the past, and, due to the nation's continued urbanization and the resultant social complexity, this trend will undoubtedly continue during future decades. The sociologist Max Weber, who contributed the word *charisma* to the behavioristic vocabulary, also coined the term *life-style*.[1] Such terms, however, mean different things to different people. As the consideration of personal life-styles, or behavioral patterns, becomes a more distinct component in social studies education, it is vital that students attain an adequate comprehension of the common terminology used by behaviorists.

In the human social order, an individual's life-style is not simply a unique or personal pattern of behavior. Rather, it is influenced by the individual's relationships with various groups and direct participation in others. Interaction with various groups, therefore, is the most significant determinant of individual behavior. Furthermore, the predictability of a person's behavior has become very accurate. For instance, the life-style of an urban secondary school youth is much different from that of a retired small-town merchant. The behavior pattern of a schoolteacher or college professor differs from that of an insurance executive. The life-style of an individual very much concerned with his or her reputation in the community differs from that of one who has openly rejected the value system of the community.

Personal behavior traits also involve many aspects of life. Knowledge of how an individual reacts in one area of his life is a valid indicator of how he will react in another situation. For example, an individual's attitude toward premarital sexual relationships probably reflects the person's attitude toward divorce. An additional basic principle is that a person's behavior pattern reflects his primary interest in life. In our society, many things may be very important to an individual, such as a profession, family, children, an avocation, and so on. A distinct life-style or behavior pattern, however, is obvious when a single interest or activity continually pervades other interests or activities—an alcoholic or a drug addict are extreme examples. More positive examples would include avid football and golf enthusiasts, and relatively "full-time" fishermen, hunters, and photographers.

Individual behavior patterns also differ according to relevant sociological variables. The first serious discussions of varying life-styles resulted from studies of

49

social stratification based upon monetary status. Karl Marx, for instance, believed that the only determinant of a person's life-style was his relationship to the means of production and consumption in a society. According to Marx, therefore, personal behavior is motivated by economic status. Research by behavioral scientists, however, suggests that similar economic levels do not motivate similar life-styles but, rather, people sharing the same general level of social prestige usually possess common behavior characteristics. In contemporary American society, many groups and, thus, many life-styles, exist. The basic sociological variables which determine these behavioristic traits are age, sex, religion, ethnicity, and residence.[2]

SEX EDUCATION AND THE SEXUAL REVOLUTION

Secondary school youth, in common with all other age groups of American society beyond the primary grades, have been, are currently, and will continue to be bombarded by the national media—movies, television, books, magazines, newspapers, advertisements, and so on. For over a decade, materials describing, portraying, and illuminating every imaginable facet of human sexuality have literally flooded the market. Regardless of intermittent legislative actions, both at the federal and the state levels, to lend perspective to this situation (whether such legislation has or lacks merit is not the issue of this discussion), this trend, which strongly suggests that society is in the midst of a liberalization of sexual standards which is altering human values, attitudes, and behavior characteristics, will undoubtedly continue indefinitely. Within the pages alloted to the discussion of this topic, it would be impossible to even list the titles of the many books designed to improve both the mental attitude toward sex and the physical capabilities to perform sex that have been published. As all educators are aware, these titles for the sophisticates of human sexuality run the gamut from such books as *Super Marriage—Super Sex, Sex and the Single Girl,* and *The Sensual Male* to such accounts as *The Art of Sensual Massage* and *The Happy Hooker.* To enumerate the current "over twenty-one" or "adults only" publications and visuals which lucidly portray the many aspects of the sexual revolution in contemporary American society would be a bibliographical impossibility. The major concern of many educators, behavioral scientists, and parents, however, is not the publication and distribution of such items, but rather—what with the ready availability of these materials to youth during their psychologically and physiologically formative years—the ensuing effects such publications will have upon the development of value systems, behavior patterns, and physical and emotional health. Largely as a result of this professional and parental concern, the phenomenon of human sexuality (in deference to human reproduction) has become an integral part of the American educational structure.

Sex Education Programs

One of the most controversial and bitterly contested domestic issues to confront the public schools since the inception of public education in the United States involves the problem of whether or not the curriculum should include systematic structured instruction in sex education. Furthermore, the particular nature of this debate will probably continue during the foreseeable future. Although the social studies is not the only curricular field to be affected by this issue, it will probably become more directly responsible for instruction in this area than any other secondary program, especially as the behavioral science subjects continue to gain increased significance.

The proponents of a systematic instructional program of sex education base their case upon a synthesis of the following arguments: Sex education is as vital to the nation's youth as education in the areas of English, the traditional social studies, the humanities, the biological and physical sciences, and mathematics.[3] The opponents of sex education base their opposition on the premise that such instruction will result in a breakdown of the Judeo-Christian or Puritanical ethic of morality among youth and will encourage more premarital sexual experimentation, a higher rate of venereal disease, more illegitimate children, more sexual "deviance," and so on, than currently exists.

Discussing Human Sexuality in Class

The foremost problem confronting social studies teachers when discussing sex as a normal human function is not the difficulty of being aware of new knowledge or the problem of content selection, but, rather, the fear and/or ignorance involved in presenting the materials. It would be difficult to discover anything really new in the field of sex education. Permissive segments of American society have permitted the availability of everything from sophisticated marriage manuals to extremely eccentric pornography. Most educational publishers, however, produce numerous instructional materials which stop short of discussing or analyzing the real issues in human sexual behavior. Indeed, if there is justification for sex education in secondary schools, there is justification for both the publication of realistic sources and the practical and realistic use of these materials in classroom instruction.

"The Sexual Revolution": A Realistic Appraisal

Regardless of the hopes and fears of educators and parents, the evidence overwhelmingly supports the premise that secondary school youth and young adults of the mid-1970s readily accept premarital sex, extramarital sex, homosexuality, group sex, and other forms of sexual behavior to a much greater degree than did previous generations. Furthermore, since the publication of Kinsey's landmark nationwide study of human sexual behavior in 1953,[4] all available

research indicates that the proportion of youth and adults participating in various forms of sexual behavior interpreted as "immoral" by the Judeo-Christian Puritanical ethic continues to increase. If the innumerable studies done on human sexual behavior are more valid than nonvalid (and there is little reason to doubt that they are), then the sexual behavior of a substantial segment of American society since mid-century is being interpreted by some behavioral scientists as a "revolution" when compared to the first half of the present century. According to this view, not only is the proportion of society engaged in such behavior larger, but the casual nature with which such behavior takes place and is discussed further reinforces the correctness of the term *sexual revolution.* [5] In contrast to this belief is the premise which holds that the popular notion that America is undergoing a sexual revolution is a myth. This view further contends that the belief that our more permissive sexual code is a sign of a general breakdown of morality is also a myth. These two myths have arisen in part because we have so little reliable information about American sexual behavior. [6]

Regardless of the relativity implied by the term *sexual revolution,* it would be the height of naiveté to suspect that today's secondary school youth are not aware of the openness with which sexual behavioral patterns are viewed, discussed, and commercially promoted. For this reason, topics dealing with human sexuality must be presented in a manner which is as objective or nonemotional as possible. If not introduced and discussed in a realistic perspective, classes in sex education for today's youth would be best omitted from the curriculum.

Premarital Sexual Patterns

Premarital sex, a misnomer for all sexual behavior engaged in by those who are not married, continues to be the most widely discussed area of all heterosexual relations and, undoubtedly, provides the most significant rationale for sex education in the American school. A steadily growing undercurrent of public and professional concern that the school system should assume more responsibility for education in this area has been evident ever since the influential Kinsey Report observed, in 1953, that about 70 percent of American males and 40 percent of the female population engage in premarital intercourse and, therefore, that society is in the throes of a sexual revolution. To offset these concerns, however, has been a dissenting viewpoint which contends that what we have experienced during the last two decades or so is merely liberalization in the public discussion of sexual behavior, thus making it appear that various types of sexual practices are more prevalent. Nevertheless, proponents of the former view have supported their case with more objective evidence. [7]

The increase in premarital sexual behavior will continue to be a matter of concern to parents and youth. However, as educators view the long-term trend toward greater premarital permissiveness, they must recognize that simply turning back the clock and reinstituting unquestioning adherence to previous norms of sexual conduct cannot be reflected in today's classroom instruction. Success in sex education can only be attained if educators, as well as parents, abandon their negative and authoritarian prohibitions on premarital sexual activity. Secondary-age youth are increasingly knowledgeable, even sophisticated, about sexual matters. As this knowledge increases, adult-induced guilt feelings (whether such approaches are attempted in or out of the classroom) will diminish substantially.

The widespread availability of acceptable birth-control techniques, greater liberalization of laws affecting abortion, and more adequate medical treatment of venereal disease have resulted in an irrevocable change in the likely consequences of (and attitudes toward) premarital relations. Teachers responsible for such instruction must realize that youth are aware that most of the problems involved in the liberation of individuals from the heritage of their fear and guilt complexes regarding sex are profoundly dependent upon medical technology's complete triumph over the probability of unwanted pregnancy. This problem will soon be solved.

It would seem that the major objective of sex education in secondary schools must be that of promoting a positively oriented sexual ethic among youth which is based upon the importance of a holistic approach to interpersonal relationships. Rather than being subjected to negative authoritarian prohibitions regarding premarital sexual activity, youth deserve the benefit of instructional strategies and inquiry techniques which encourage them to make individual decisions concerning what they should do about premarital intercourse. This decision-making technique should be based upon what types of personal behavior would improve their relationships with others, rather than on a standard of absolute right or wrong interpersonal behavior in terms of social mores, taboos, or abstract logic. However a particular community defines sexual morality at a particular time, this standard must be "sold" to youth on some modern and practical—yet at the same time idealistic—basis, and not be rooted in older metaphysical or theological concepts which are out of synchronization with present-day reality.

In all facets of personal behavior, youth desire guidance, either overtly or covertly. Indeed, if enlightened guidance is needed, why isn't it provided? Even from casual observation, it seems reasonable to speculate that one reason teachers and parents fail to provide the guidance in sexual matters that youth desire is that they are confused by the apparent inapplicability of many older codes and conventions to the realities of space-age living. For many youth, the traditional has become suspect. This continues to result in a value and attitudinal conflict on the part of students, and causes even more concern for many teachers who would like to preserve something of our cultural heritage of sexual morality, yet at the same time don't want to appear old-fashioned or "square" by sternly denouncing all premarital sexual activity.

In social studies methods courses for in-service teachers, this writer has had some degree of success in designing the following instructional strategy for presenting various topics within the controversial theme of sex education. Both teachers and students should collect data and analyze the hypothesis that some of the same technological and social innovations which have conditioned our society continually to consider the value of change itself in a positive context, have also contributed to the decreasing significance of traditional customs concerning many aspects of human behavior, including sexual activity. Some of these innovations directly affecting sexual behavior would include cross-class associations resulting from urbanism, better contraceptive devices, liberalized abortion laws, improved venereal-disease control, and the commercial glorification of sex. All of these have contributed to the demotion of premarital sexual chastity from its former status as a highly ranked cultural value. For instance, one need look no further than some current marriage-relations books, which include sections on "positive values of premarital intercourse," to visualize how the technological revolution has influenced this element of the social revolution in an advanced nation like the United States.

Obviously, such an approach will force students to acknowledge a great deal of confusion and insecurity, but at the same time it should promote their ability to resolve or compromise any potential emotional conflict resulting from sexual behavior. The instructional guidelines for this technique are based upon the psychological premise that human emotional nature comprises conflicting drives which can be adjusted outside the perspective of absolutist good or bad behavior. Teachers must instill within students that rational man is becoming aware that he lives a life of rehearsing in imagination the hopeless war between his physiological impulses and his social aspirations.[8] Rather, psychological and sociological research strongly indicates that mankind is becoming equally aware that there is no way for a human to grow and mature without acknowledging the conflicts of life and accepting full responsibility for living with them and improving the ability to maintain a high level of emotional health.[9]

Throughout any discussion of premarital sexual relations, however, it is vital for the instructor to always be aware that no widely acceptable "modern" standard of sexual behavior has been defined. There is no absolute standard indicating the acceptable limits of premarital permissiveness, nor is it likely that there will be such during the foreseeable future.

Homosexuality and Bisexuality

Since the late 1960s, the phenomena of male and female homosexuality and bisexuality in American society have been the subjects of an ever-increasing amount of medical and academic review and research. Furthermore, all evidence indicates that these forms of sexual behavior—which, among a large segment of society, are considered to be forms of deviant behavior—will continue to receive more and more systematic examination from behavioral scientists in future years. As with other forms of human sexuality, the growing attention given to homosexuality and bisexuality merits conscientious analysis in any program of sex education.

Two conclusions resulting from the findings of numerous surveys involving sexuality which have been conducted in secondary schools and on college campuses during the past decade would suggest that American youth view these behaviors in a somewhat paradoxical situation. On the one hand, the majority regard these activities as examples of deviant behavior; at the same time, the majority reveal a much more liberal attitude of tolerance or acceptance for individuals who choose these life-styles, as compared with attitudes expressed by youth of previous generations.[10] Regarding homosexuality and bisexuality as more acceptable forms of personal life-style than during the immediate past is probably a result of the awareness on the part of youth that both patterns of sexual behavior are increasing in our society, as well as becoming more overt or visible. In addition, homosexuality and bisexuality have been forbidden subjects for classroom discussion at the secondary education level until fairly recently in the United States. During the late 1960s and early 1970s, however, books reaching the best-seller list, as well as movies and plays, television and newspapers, have continually portrayed homosexuality and bisexuality in more realistic perspective.

Homosexual Behavior Patterns

The collecting of reliable data concerning the numbers and distribution of male homosexuals in American society continues to be seriously hindered by the forces of social taboo. The continued subjugation of male homosexuals (to a greater degree than lesbians) to police harassment, legal punishments, employment problems, and social condemnation has resulted in a complex structure of concealed social relations. Nevertheless, there is valid evidence which strongly suggests that there are millions of exclusively homosexual males distributed throughout every geographical region of the nation and throughout every socioeconomic stratum.[11] One of the most current estimates of the number of males who are exclusively homosexual is placed at over 4 million. This figure would probably be much higher if the number of males who were committed more to homosexual relations than to heterosexual relations could be accurately determined.[12] Indeed, if practicing lesbians were included in these statistics, reliable estimates then would place the number of male and female homosexuals in the United States at approximately 25 million, or more than 10 percent of the nation's population.[13] In the near future, however, due to recent developments of national significance, the collection of reliable data on the number of males who are exclusively homosexual, as well as some of the psychological and sociological insights as to why they choose this life-style, will be easier to attain.

By way of significant distinctions between male and female homosexual behavior patterns, secondary youth are probably also aware that society's attitude toward male homosexuality is much more strict than its attitude toward lesbian life-styles. Society is manifestly more concerned with repressing and sanctioning male homosexuality than with repressing female homosexuals. Although a variety of reasons have been offered for this attitudinal difference, the severity of the sanctions against the male is probably due to the level of social anxiety induced by male homosexuality (due largely to the traditional concept of the cultural role of the male in society) in contrast to female homosexuality. For example, the nationwide gay liberation movement is, in effect, a revolutionary movement organized by male rather than female homosexuals.

Bisexual Behavior Patterns

Recent evidence reveals that a small but apparently growing number of Americans are practicing bisexuality, an age-old but still largely mysterious behavior pattern that is only just beginning to be subjected to the scrutiny of scientific investigation. Even though a few individuals have publicly proclaimed their sexual interest in both males and females, the vast majority of bisexuals, like homosexuals, remain underground. Unlike many exclusive homosexuals, many of these persons are married. Like members of the homosexual community, however, they fear that disclosure of their sexual activities would result in social condemnation and economic reprisals. Similarly, bisexuality occurs in all walks and levels of economic and social life.[14] Data concerning the number of bisexuals in American society are not accurate; at most they are believed to comprise a small, though steadily increasing, segment of the population. Furthermore, it is believed that most of the increase in bisexual behavior is among women rather than men, partly for political reasons, such as a feminine-liberating phenomenon as they disassociate themselves from the extraordinary dependence they have traditionally had on the male.

Aside from such tentative observations, there is little evidence available to draw valid conclusions regarding the number of bisexual individuals or the personal reasons for bisexual behavior. What can be stated with validity, however, is that while bisexuality is the largest remaining mystery in the field of human sexuality, its practice will continue to increase.

The Study of Homosexuality and Bisexuality

It is imperative that programs in sex education in the American secondary school be revised to include the depiction of male and female homosexuality and bisexuality as existing behavioral patterns and life-styles for a relatively small, but apparently ever-growing, proportion of our society. The framework for the introduction and presentation of these extremely controversial topics in social studies classes should be organized around changing behavioral patterns in a technologically advanced society. For instance, evidence exists that when a society becomes progressively more urbanized and more complex technologically, as ours is doing, it becomes more difficult for the male to strictly define and fulfill the traditional masculine cultural role, as exemplified by the continually growing proportion of women in all segments of the labor force, and by the intensity of the women's liberation movement and its major cause of promoting affirmative action for females in all sectors of the economy.

In classroom discussions of male and female homosexuality, it would seem that every effort must be made to relate the concepts of "normal" and "deviant" sexual behavior to the value systems of society. For example, since societal values and attitudinal systems are constantly in the process of evaluation and change, students should be encouraged to examine the premise that some of the sexual patterns currently considered deviant may not be regarded as such in the near future.

Additional techniques which can be utilized to present a more objective view of homosexual behavior should utilize the findings of several very current and exhaustive studies of the male homosexual in the United States and the technologically advanced nations of Western Europe.[15] In the writer's opinion, the conclusions of these new research studies strongly suggest that the psychological or emotional health of male homosexuals is as good as that of heterosexual males, and that homosexuals should end their tradition of silence. Furthermore, the conclusions of these studies recommend the end of laws and harassment directed against consenting adult homosexuals. The introduction of such material as this in social education should be related to other recent developments designed to remove the social barriers from an individual's sexual behavior. Specifically, the writer believes that students should be aware of the recent decision of the influential American Psychiatric Association, in December 1973, to remove homosexuality from its list of mental illnesses. This revolutionary action was followed in August 1973, by the American Bar Association, which proposed the resolution: "Resolved, that the legislatures of the several states are urged to repeal all laws which classify as criminal conflict any form of non-commercial sexual conduct between consenting adults in private, saving only those portions which protect minors or public decorum."[16] Two states, Illinois and Colorado, have enacted such legislation. In addition, students should be asked to carefully analyze the primary reasons or rationale for the actions of these two national professional groups. With regard to classroom discussions of bisexual behavior, it has been long established that all humans are bisexual in the sense that they are able to respond sexually to some degree toward people of either sex. Current research indicates that most bisexuals are either predominantly homosexual or predominantly heterosexual. The writer feels that students should be asked to reflect upon some of the possible reasons why an individual is motivated to engage in this type of sexual activity.

In any discussion of human sexuality, however, it is absolutely vital that social studies teachers provide students with the awareness that many responsible social and behavioral scientists firmly believe that the absolute number of male and female homosexuals and bisexuals is not as great as is many times suggested and, furthermore, that the number of individuals who engage in such sexual practices is, in fact, declining relatively in relation to the increase in population growth.

In addition, many experts express the opinion that sexual behavior which results only in physical gratification is being replaced by the widespread attitude that homosexual and bisexual practices do not result in the satisfying emotional attachments which are afforded by heterosexual relationships. Also, this group believes that many of the individuals who have glorified and encouraged extremely liberal forms of sexual experimentation are rapidly achieving the realization that emotional health can only be maintained through heterosexual unions.

Obscenity-Pornography Issues

As noted at the outset of this discussion, books, magazines, films, and various paraphernalia depicting and glorifying every imaginable form of human sexual behavior and fantasy are readily available to today's youth of secondary school age. There appear to be two fundamental questions which should serve as the basis for discussions of pornography in the secondary classroom. First, do such erotic stimuli sexually excite and arouse youth of this age group? Second, and perhaps most significant, does such exposure affect the present and subsequent sexual behavior of youth? Indeed, the first question is much easier to answer.

During the past decade, numerous research studies have been conducted in which attempts were made to determine the relationship between pornographic or erotic materials and personal sexual behavior. Paralleling these individual and institutional studies were the extensive experiments conducted by the highly controversial but influential President's Commission on Obscenity, which reported its findings in 1972.[17] Most of these studies had one common theme. They attempted to determine, through the use of sophisticated research techniques, whether there is a positive correlation between exposure to pornographic materials and the committing of sex acts which are considered to be criminal; for example, rape, child molestation, and so on. The samples used in these research studies included, by age group, adolescents, young adults, middle-aged individuals, and older people, both male and female. The additional major variable was to investigate the impact of erotic materials upon the sexual criminal and the noncriminal by age group. The findings of these studies, including the conclusions of the President's Commission on Obscenity, have been inconclusive.

An excellent instructional technique for introducing the topic of pornography and obscenity in sex education courses is to assign individual students, or groups of students, the task of examining and reporting on both the research design and the findings of current studies involving the relationship between erotic stimuli and personal sexual behavior. From such analysis, students should become aware of many of the difficulties confronting behavioral and social scientists in their attempts to establish a significant relationship between pornography and sexual behavior.

A second, but closely related, instructional activity would be to promote student awareness of the many complex problems involved in the defining of pornographic or obscene materials. Student inquiry into this issue should consist of thorough analysis of recent (since 1970) Supreme Court statements and decisions concerning obscene materials,[18] as well as definitions and decisions of particular state and community judicial and legislative bodies.

A third significant area for student investigation concerns the questions involved in the legalization of pornography for commercial distribution. For example, individual students might examine recent legislation in several West European nations concerning legalized pornography, as well as the apparent reasons for such action. Also, the rationale for the divergent obscenity opinions of the United States Supreme Court since 1972 would provide a most relevant albeit difficult topic for student research.

Such classroom projects should provide students with a better insight into the extremely complex social and legal issues involved in the pornography and obscenity question. Furthermore, the examination of these problems should reinforce student awareness that, like all questions concerning modern morality, the many questions related to definitions of pornography, the relationships between obscene materials and personal sexual behavior, and the issues involved in the legalization of pornography, will continue to be questions of social significance to which no explicit or absolute right or wrong answers will be expressed or accepted universally.

The extremely controversial nature of sex education emerges when both advocates and opponents become involved in the continual debate concerning such topics as what constitutes morality, sexual perversion, pornography and the emotional and psychological effects of pornography, as well as the diverse psychological theories concerning controlled versus complete sexual freedom—in essence, the lack of universally accepted values or attitudes about what constitutes psychologically and physiologically good or bad sexual behavior, to say nothing of the relativity involved in the issues of what is right or wrong, or what is normal or abnormal, in terms of sexual conduct. This latter situation is underscored by the fact that psychological and psychiatric experts are divided on nearly every issue concerning human sexual behavior.

The social studies teacher who is or may be responsible for sex education instruction should be aware of several major considerations. First, this subject is probably the most emotional of all the controversial issues in contemporary public education. Second, sex education materials contain an extremely wide range of relativity, and descriptive, absolute, and final answers will be impossible to structure. Third, the accepted societal attitudes toward sexual behavior will, in many instances, vary considerably in different areas of the nation, with the most significant variance existing between rural communities and larger urban areas. Likewise, sexual mores will vary between where the students are presently attending secondary school and where many of them will move to attend college, to work, or to spend their adult lives. Finally, the teacher must attempt to be as objective as possible, using the best evidence and instructional materials he can acquire, and should be prepared to defend his position and methods before administrative officers of the school system, parents, community civic and religious groups, and lay representatives of the general public.

Every major social change, whether or not it can be termed a revolution, involves a basic shift in human values and behavior. The social studies teacher must be aware that the conservative segment of society, which holds to the traditional values, sees not change but decadence. In essence, it appears to these people that others—and, in this instance, young people—have given up on the traditional virtues and are accepting life-styles which are of no value and will lead to both individual and social destruction. With comparable inevitability, those who accept new social values and life-styles view them as replacing outmoded values and consider them positive with regard to both the individual and society. It is within this context that the social studies teacher must attempt to deal with the many and varied attitudes that will be reflected in sex education instruction.

In conclusion, while courses in sex education cannot determine whether or not youth will think about sexual behavior, such instruction can significantly influence the perspective in which they consider human sexuality. Regardless of what a highly conservative segment of society believes about such instruction, expanding patterns of sexual activity will increase during the future. The foremost objective of sex education should be to foster the understanding among youth that sexuality is a healthy and joyous part of life.

Assumptions for Student Inquiry

1. Both the proponents and opponents of sex education in the schools have the same ultimate goal in mind regarding instruction about human sexual conduct: that of attempting to preserve the basic attitudes toward sexual behavior as interpreted by the Judeo-Christian ethic and social tradition.
2. The current rise in the rates of venereal disease and illegitimate children among young people is probably due, for the most part, to a combination of three factors: (1) the widespread availability and use of oral contraceptives, (2) the present relative liberalization of attitudes toward sexual behavior, and (3) the anonymity afforded by increased urbanization.
3. What types of materials constitute pornography, and the legal penalties for distributing, transporting, and possessing such materials, in the view of the court system and as interpreted by the law, has been, and probably will continue to be, cyclic in nature, based upon a liberal versus conservative interpretation of the definition of pornography as well as the laws affecting such materials.
4. Throughout its history the United States has witnessed, in a legal sense, an evolutionary, liberalizing attitude toward the distribution and possession of pornographic materials, as well as more liberal interpretations of what constitutes such materials.
5. Within one decade there will probably be no sexual materials which, in a legal sense, will be considered pornographic in nature.
6. An ever-increasing proportion of American society probably will continue to portray a more liberal attitude toward the types of sexual conduct that are considered sexual deviance or perversion among many segments of society.

7. Although laws and legislation will remain necessary to protect the young, it is highly possible that within one to two decades in the United States, no form of human sexual behavior between consenting adults will legally or socially be considered to constitute sexual perversion.

8. Sex education instruction in the public schools, organized and taught by competent individuals, will result in a substantial decrease in the rates of both venereal disease and illegitimate children among young people.

9. Much of the fear and guilt associated with sexual behavior—which, in many instances, results in serious and lifelong emotional disturbance—would be alleviated if all secondary students could experience competent instruction in the mental and physical aspects of human sexuality.

10. Competent instruction in sex education during the adolescent years would result in a substantial decrease in the divorce rate in the United States.

11. The fact that we now refer to sexual "deviations" rather than to "perversions" is evidence that our society is beginning to accept more readily the reality of homosexuals and bisexuals.

12. In patterns of human sexual behavior, there continues to exist a wide difference in interpretation between professional opinion and social opinion.

13. The attitude that premarital sex is always immoral has for years been a minority view; among today's youth, it is a view that is practically extinct.

14. Laws designed to promote or prohibit particular types of sexual behavior patterns should be abolished.

15. Western civilization will not continue to exist if homosexuality is legalized.

16. Enough exhaustive research has been done to conclude that the extensive viewing of pornographic or obscene materials will result in abnormal or even criminal sexual behavior.

17. There appears to be no positive relationship between pornography and criminal sexual behavior.

18. It will remain impossible to provide socially acceptable definitions of pornography, abnormal sexual behavior, or normal sexual behavior.

MARRIAGE, FAMILY DISINTEGRATION, AND DIVORCE

During the last half-century, the trend of divorce rates in the United States has continued to increase. Currently, the nationwide average is approximately 40 percent, although the divorce rate in some metropolitan areas is approaching 70 percent.[19] Significantly, all available evidence indicates that the divorce rate will continue to increase throughout the foreseeable future. Thus, for two vital reasons it is vital that social studies teachers be knowledgeable of this behavioral trend and its many societal implications: first, divorce will continue to be a basic social issue in the United States; and second, a significant proportion of the students currently attending the secondary schools will both marry and divorce.

Students should understand that an increase in the divorce rate does not necessarily imply that there are more unhappy marriages than previously. Such an increase could indicate that more couples are able to afford divorce, socially and economically, and, therefore, are dissolving more marriages than previously. Additionally, while the increase in the divorce rate represents an increase in the number of legally dissolved marriages, it may be that the increase in divorce is counterbalanced by a drop in desertions. There are no adequate figures available on desertion.[20] In the past, when it was more difficult to obtain a divorce, and when the financial fee for divorce was much higher, the only available alternatives for the lower-income man were to remain unhappily married or desert. Obviously, desertion rates were much higher in the past than now, due to the ease of obtaining a divorce, the reduced legal fees, and the extreme difficulty of deserting one's family without paying an extreme financial penalty.

Reasons for Divorce

Attempting to explain to students the reasons why a marriage fails is as difficult as attempting to explain the causes of war.[21] Strained relations and increasing hostility continue to perpetuate a situation which finally becomes so intolerable for one or both individuals that divorce appears to be the only solution.

Contrary to the belief among adolescents (as well as many adults), there is no absolute point at which a marriage falls apart. There may be a sudden recognition that something is extremely wrong, but it is usually the result of a repression that has been developing for a considerable period. Indeed, some marriages are failures from the beginning. The transition from the single role to the role of husband or wife is difficult to accomplish. This change of role may never be achieved, and there must be a minimum of alteration in role behavior for a marriage to survive.

Marriage and the Family in the Year 2000

Regardless of conservative segments of public opinion, and whether one is for or against such behavior, the trend toward greater freedom in sexual relationships, for both youth and adults, is very likely to increase throughout the remainder of the present century. There appears little doubt that sexual intimacy will be a common element of any continuing relationship between two individuals. Futurists also predict that the attitude of possessiveness—of dominating another person—which has traditionally characterized most sexual unions, will be largely diminished.[22] The impact of women's liberation in all social and economic sectors will probably result in sexual equality early in the last quarter of the twentieth century.

Significantly, it can be accurately predicted that there need not be any children resulting from sexual union in one or two decades unless desired. By one of the several techniques currently in experimental stages, each individual, while still in early adolescence, can be assured of continued infertility. Contrary to the present situation, where positive action is needed to prevent contraception, it will necessitate positive action to reestablish fertility. In adition, tremendous strides will be made in the improvement of computerized matching of prospective partners with compatible characteristics.

By the conclusion of the present century, many of the temporary unions formed by members of the opposite sex may be legalized, but in a much different form of marriage from what we know today. Public pressure is presently forcing such types of unions, where there will be no permanent commitment, no children (by mutual consent), and, if the marriage is dissolved, no need for showing legal cause and no alimony. All available evidence indicates that male-female relationships will have permanance only to the degree in which they satisfy the emotional, psychological, intellectual, and physical needs of the partners. Furthermore, if children are not permitted in such marriages, then the rate of one in two marriages ending in divorce (the current rate in the state of California as well as other sections of the country) will not constitute a human tragedy. On the basis of these predictions, students might examine the hypothesis that the probability for a congenial and rewarding permanent marriage in the future will be better than now and in the past, since many causes of the current divorce rate will have been solved during the long period of the nonlegalized marriage union.

Introducing Marriage

Secondary students should be encouraged to collect data concerning marriage since they will be in the midst of innumerable alterations in the legal and social aspects of this behavior pattern throughout their adult lives. Some of the more notable predictions are mentioned below.

In 1927, John B. Watson, the psychologist, prophesied that by 1977, or four decades hence, marriage would no longer exist, for by then family standards would have completely broken down and the automobile and other things would have taken the child out of control.[23] In 1937, Peter Sorokin, the sociologist, prophesied that divorce and separation would increase until any profound difference between socially sanctioned marriages and illicit sex relations disappeared. The home would become a mere overnight parking place, devoted mainly to sexual relationships.[24]

As has been predicted by sociologists and social scientists, vast changes in family structure are occurring, and will continue to occur, in response to societal change. The conditions which have produced these social changes involved technological development, urbanization, moderation of religious attitudes, and ideological change. Most evidence suggests that social change will continue at an even more rapid rate in the future, thus increasing the shifts in the structure of social institutions, such as marriage and the traditional family structure.[25] Indeed, it has been pointed out that the faster the rate of social change and the longer the life span, the greater the increase in the statistical odds against an indefinitely lasting love of one person expressed through the conventional marriage relationship, and it is the statistical odds against love that account for the high divorce and separation rates in technological societies.[26]

Prophesizing about these issues in *Future Shock,* Alvin Toffler examines the future of the family in what he projects as the super-industrial society which we are rapidly approaching in the United States. Among his conclusions, Toffler predicts that the family institution will not disappear but is likely instead to evolve into a variety of forms. One specific change he expects is the redefinition of parenthood in a technological era when science will make it possible to purchase an embryo with any desired set of physical and mental characteristics. Obviously this makes geriatric parenthood a most realistic possibility. Childlessness may become more common in response to the need for a very mobile family, and many couples may have their children raised by "professional parents." Communal family arrangements may result in an effort to offset the loneliness accompanying transience. Families may come to include such things as a single unmarried parent and children, polygamous marriages, and homosexual marriages. With a high rate of social change and increased longevity, the odds are that the traditional concept of love and marriage will become less common.[27]

Other futurists have recently arrived at similar conclusions concerning these issues. For instance, trial marriage and serial polygamy will legitimize, while group marriages, homosexual marriages, and unmarried parenthood will be socially condoned. Thus, the evidence of prediction indicates that the social systems characterized by intimate interaction and sexual contact will continue to proliferate. Indeed, it is possible that the individual of the future will experience the duality of traditional dating and marriage, serial marriages, adultery, communal sex, communal child-rearing, homosexual relationships, and a variety of other personal life-styles.[28]

It would seem vital that social studies teachers provide opportunities for students to become involved in discussions of these social issues for the following primary reasons: (1) Regardless of support from organized religion, business and industry, and the vast majority of society, the total institution of marriage in American society is gravely ill. Vance Packard, in *The Sexual Wilderness,* summarizes from recent surveys that "a marriage made in the United States in the late 1960's has about a 50:50 chance of remaining even nominally intact."[29] By the early 1970s, the odds on success had decreased more. (2) Closely related is the "fact" that the American family, as we have known it, is slowly disintegrating. Evidence of its collapse is visible in the multitude of unhappy, broken families and miserable people. However, new family forms are evolving from the ruins of the monogamous structure, forms which will undoubtedly affect many of today's secondary school students.

Assumptions for Student Inquiry

1. Regardless of its many shortcomings and high rate of failure, the traditional heterosexual marriage union is the best means for preserving social stability and promoting the emotional security and maturity of the individual.
2. Due to the continued growth of social and economic technology and urbanization, the complexities confronting the human condition in the United States will result in a continued rise in the divorce rate during the future. Furthermore, increased

family disintegration is a direct result of technological development in all advanced nations.

3. By the end of the present century, the institution of the traditional heterosexual marriage may have broken down, to the extent that more adults will either be single or living by polygamous or trial marriages than in the traditional marriage union.

4. A partial solution to the increasing divorce rate in the United States would be for the federal, state, and local governments to enact laws raising the legal age of marriage to thirty years for males and twenty-five years for females.

5. In addition, if the only grounds for divorce were adultery, the rate of divorce would be reduced drastically and society and the individual would benefit enormously.

6. The only solution to the emotionally unhappy condition which characterizes such a high proportion of today's marriages is to legally institute trial heterosexual marriages, trial polygamous marriages, and trial homosexual marriages.

7. In an attempt to reduce the increasing divorce rate, married and single adults should be emotionally and legally free from any restrictions regarding sexual relations with other individuals of either sex.

8. The state—that is, governmental bodies and legal agencies at all levels—should have no influence in determining the legality of marriage, divorce, family structures, or adult sexual relationships.

9. Due to the increasing life span and the earlier age of death among married men than married women, resulting in so many widows and fatherless children, it should be enacted that the male be five to ten years younger than the female for a marriage to be legalized.

10. With regard to matters involving trial, polygamous, and homosexual marriages, divorce, communal families, and sexual relations, as well as other areas of the human condition, it is a basic truism that minorities experiment and majorities cling to the past.

ALCOHOLISM AND DRUG ABUSE EDUCATION

Although alcoholism and drug abuse are not considered to be strictly within the academic limits of the secondary social studies, there is little doubt that they will continue to receive more attention in such classes than in any other major curricular area. When promoting discussions on these topics, as with other controversial issues, the social studies instructor must develop the dialogue around the relative aspects of the drug abuse situation in the United States, rather than introducing scare tactics. Furthermore, the instructor should not attempt to expound absolute negative or positive answers concerning drug use.

Alcoholism Among American Youth

The proportion of adults who consume alcohol is presently at the highest point recorded in thirty-five years of regular Gallup audits of America's drinking habits. In the latest survey, 68 percent of Americans over the age of eighteen (or a projected 95 million persons) report that they have occasion to consume alcoholic beverages.[30] Another national organization, the National Clearinghouse of

Alcoholics Anonymous, states that about 95 million Americans over fifteen years of age drink with some regularity. Of these, an estimated 9 million are alcoholics or problem drinkers, compared with 5 million ten years ago.[31]

The significance of these statistics for the secondary education curriculum is that the use of alcohol apparently is surpassing the use of other drugs among the nation's teenagers. The second report of the President's National Commission on Marijuana and Drug Abuse stated: "Among junior high, senior high and college students, alcohol is, by far, the drug of choice. . . . 56 percent of the junior high students, 75 percent of the senior high students, and 83 percent of the college students have used alcohol at least once."[32] Corroborating this recent evidence, a national survey conducted by the Commission on Marijuana and Drug Abuse reported that "6 million teenagers said they drank liquor, compared with 3.5 million teenagers who said they smoked marijuana."[33] In addition, the director of the Department of Health, Education and Welfare's National Institute on Alcoholism recently commented that "youth are moving from a wide range of other drugs to the most devastating drug—the one most widely misused of all—alcohol."[34]

There is some evidence that educational systems throughout the nation are placing more emphasis upon alcohol education in the curriculum. It would seem an effective strategy for instructors responsible for teaching about alcoholism and alcohol-related issues to organize classroom discussions around the general problem of mental health and, thus, encourage students to examine some of the basic underlying causes why young people begin to consume alcohol in the first place. Obviously, the traditional judgmental, abstinence-oriented approach has not been successful and must be replaced by more realistic instructional techniques.

Drug Abuse Trends

Although the use of marijuana continues on a substantial basis among youth, there is considerable evidence to suggest that the use of "hard" drugs (heroin and many of the amphetamine drugs) among secondary school students and young adults is decreasing notably.[35] Among the reasons that have been offered to explain this declining trend is the widespread awareness among youth of the devastating effects of hard drugs—deaths resulting from overdoses, the visual human tragedy of addiction, and the harsh legal penalties for using or selling drugs.[36] The results of marijuana use, nevertheless, continue to be open to debate, based upon continued research efforts. Currently, however, most of the evidence suggests that the abuse of marijuana will result in a negative effect upon the human physiological system.

In addition, it has been suggested that the highly negative societal attitude toward the use of hard drugs has contributed significantly to this decline. This situation, however, has resulted in an increase of alcohol consumption, as discussed above, and underscored by one expert when he stated that "alcohol is the socially accepted drug in our society, really the socially accepted drug of the world."[37]

Like instructional strategies designed to teach about alcohol and alcoholism, the organizing concept for drug education should emphasize the value of developing positive mental health and self-esteem on the part of youth. Young people who are instilled with a feeling of value and meaningful purpose to their lives are not nearly as prone to use or abuse drugs. An additional approach for promoting an objective discussion of this topic in social studies classes is to have students compare the abuse of drugs to the use and abuse of alcohol in American society. Such a discussion would involve three major themes for student consideration. First, to what extent does peer or social pressure initiate the use of drugs or alcohol among junior and senior high school students? Second, since the problems of alcohol and drug abuse appear to be symptoms, what appear to be the basic causes which produce such symptoms? Third, will the use of soft drugs (marijuana) eventually become legal in the same respect as the use of alcohol?

By developing instructional techniques around these and similar themes, the social studies teacher is involving students in those areas of human concern in which he or she possesses a relatively high level of competence, namely, in the behavior patterns of individuals. It must be emphasized that the classroom teacher should not become involved in the physiological and psychological aspects of either drug or alcohol abuse. When these concomitant dimensions of drug usage are to be considered, it is imperative that individuals competent in these fields be invited as guest consultants.

Assumptions for Student Inquiry

1. In many instances, the high rate of alcohol and drug abuse on the part of today's youth is the result of the extreme parental and social pressure exerted upon youth beyond their innate abilities.
2. The complexity of life brought about by the stress of continued urbanization in the United States has resulted in a lack of both family and peer security among many youth, and thus is the basic cause for drug usage and the increase in the consumption of alcohol among many young people.
3. The increasing rate of alcohol consumption among youth is due primarily to the failure of the educational system and the home to provide adequate instruction about the potential dangers to physical and mental health that excessive use of this drug may cause.
4. The increase in excessive alcohol consumption and the decline in the use of hard drugs are the result of a feeling among many youth that since the use of alcohol is legal, it is also socially acceptable.
5. The excessive use of alcohol and drugs among many youth, as well as many adults, clearly indicates that the extreme emphasis placed upon materialism and competition in technologically advanced societies such as ours results in fears and anxieties, and in a loss of the more basic values, attitudes, and behavior traits that are necessary for human beings if they are to enjoy stable, happy, and successful lives.

6. Instead of condemning the use of alcoholic beverages, drug abuse educational programs and parents should teach youth how to drink responsibly and in moderation.

MENTAL HEALTH, NEUROSIS, AND PSYCHOSIS

Running a very close second to the commercial publications involving issues of human sexuality and marriage and the family is the plethora of books designed for the general public concerning all aspects of mental health. The high marketability of such publications is evidenced by the number of new titles and variety of topics which appear continually. There would seem little doubt that there is a very positive correlation between the tremendous technological strides this nation has accomplished and the increase in emotional stress that has accompanied such material and scientific advancement. Furthermore, there is substantial evidence which suggests that the more technologically advanced and, thereby, more highly urbanized our nation becomes, the more complex social interaction and communication will become, resulting in an increasing proportion of the population which suffers some degree of emotional anxiety. One need only to observe the proportionate increase in the use of alcohol, drugs, and psychotherapy among all segments of American society during recent years to support this premise.

MENTAL HEALTH TOPICS

Societal complexity will continue to increase throughout the lives of today's secondary school students. It would appear, however, that much of what is presently termed "formal education" continues to be designed to prepare youth to function successfully in society as it existed in the past. Indeed, such "education" must be considered static in terms of the present and future needs of the nation's youth. The radically changing demands which society will place upon the individual throughout the remainder of this decade, and in future decades, will render traditional education relatively useless with regard to preparing today's student to enjoy a happy, productive, and meaningful adult life.

As noted in previous sections of this discussion, the foremost responsibility of the social studies curriculum is to prepare youth to be effective citizens within a democratic society. Obviously, therefore, any program which contributes to the physical, emotional, social, or moral development of youth contributes directly to the welfare of society. Largely for these reasons, the subjects comprising the behavioral sciences will become increasingly significant components of the social studies curriculum, since they emphasize the study of behavior patterns which directly influence the development of positive or negative mental health.

Throughout classroom discussions of mental health in our society, four major themes should continually be stressed to students. First, mental illness is a problem which is rapidly achieving more compassion and understanding in the public conscience. The social stigma which has been associated with emotional disorders is being replaced with the widespread acceptance of the attitude that people suffering from various forms of mental illness should be treated and can be cured. Second, mental health represents the single largest medical problem in the United States today. The most accurate current estimates reveal that approximately 70 percent of the patients in general hospitals alone, aside from mental institutions, have illnesses which are either psychiatric-oriented or intensified by a psychiatric problem. Third, emotional illness may strike any age group of the population, in any socioeconomic structure, at any time. It must be emphasized to students that no one is either inherently or environmentally immune from emotionally induced illness. Fourth, mental health is much more than a lack of mental illness. Mental health consists of a quality of life that is exemplified by a good, comfortable, and satisfactory feeling with one's life and his or her relationships with other individuals and groups.

In order to comprehend the complexities of human behavior as they affect mental health, students must first achieve an understanding that human beings are influenced by a number of forces, including biology, inheritance, environment, and other fundamental factors. Specifically, attention should be given to those aspects of behavior that are controlled by heredity, such as instinctual drives like the need for food and sleep. This instinctual part of the human personality is what the famed psychologist Sigmund Freud defined as the "id." Human beings are also influenced by external forces, especially by other people. Obviously, parents are usually the most significant influence, since from birth the child's physical and emotional development is dependent upon parental guidance. Through parental love, children begin a sense of individuality which Freud termed the "ego." The ego represents our conscious awareness of ourselves and includes the unique characteristic of humans, the ability to reason. In addition to the id and the ego, the child is confronted with the patterns of the environment away from the family. As children learn to adjust to the realities of the social environment, a third segment of the human personality develops, the part that Freud referred to as the "superego," which represents the values of the child's external environment, namely, society.[38] Those behaviorists who agree with the Freudian view express the thesis that our personal behavior, and the status of our emotional health as we mature, is the result of the interactions of the id, ego, and superego. In essence, the Freudian school believes that most of man's troubles result from internally generated anxieties, the product of repressed conflicting drives that alienate him from society.

At this point in such a discussion, students must become acquainted with other significant theories concerning the psychological development of humans. For example, many modern behaviorists, as exemplified by B. F. Skinner, expound an opposite point of view to that presented by Freud. These behaviorists maintain that it is not the individual, but rather the world around the individual, that is the source of most of man's problems. This viewpoint contends that our age (mid-

and late-twentieth-century man) is not suffering from anxiety, but from the accidents, crimes, wars, and other dangerous and painful things to which people are often exposed. Young people drop out of school, refuse to get jobs, and associate only with others of their own age, not because they feel alienated, but because of defective social environments in homes, schools, factories, and elsewhere.[39] In effect, these newer theories express the viewpoint that increasing social demands and the complex cultural environment significantly influence our mental health and behavior as we mature. Students should also become acquainted with a similar behaviorist school of thought which was developed by another famous psychologist, Carl Jung. This group believes that on a deeper level all humans share elements of man's past, present, and future. Jung personally maintained that without this "collective unconscious," there is no reason why the same behavior characteristics would appear in so many different time periods and places.[40]

Regardless of what particular behaviorist theories students are exposed to, or have an affinity for in relation to discussions of mental health and other behavior patterns, they should understand that there currently is widespread agreement among psychologists, psychiatrists, and behaviorists that people develop varying degrees of mental illness not necessarily because they are confronted with overwhelming amounts of trouble, but rather because they have not developed the mental abilities to cope with the numerous problems and difficulties which are common to all people. A major point to emphasize to students is that the ability to deal with the various phases of ordinary human life in an effective manner—or, in other words, in a manner which results in a maximum amount of pleasure and enjoyment with a minimum amount of mental stress—is known as "maturity." Achieving maturity, or being mature, means possessing emotional stability, which is the ability to maintain equanimity, resignation, courage, determination, and cheerfulness when a particular situation or combination of events might result in an immature individual expressing feelings of apprehension, fear, anxiety, or frustration. In short, the attainment of maturity is basic to the development of good mental health.

The development of maturity, however, is a learning process. Unfortunately, there presently is no place within the traditional educational program in general, or the social studies curriculum in particular, where youth can be provided the opportunity to learn maturity and, thereby, improve their chances for maintaining good mental health throughout their adult lives. It would seem, however, that modern social studies programs must assume responsibility for this nontraditional but essential area of education.

As a guideline for class discussions of maturity and mental health, the instructor might encourage students to analyze the following concepts. Good mental health consists of the following general characteristics:[41]

1. A positive feeling of responsibility and independence.

2. A realization that extreme aggressiveness, anger, hate, cruelty, and belligerency are human weaknesses, and that compassion, goodness, and kindness are positive characteristics.
3. The ability to distinguish reality from fantasy.
4. Possessing the ability to adjust to change with respect to residence or employment.
5. Possessing concern for others and their problems rather than a feeling of extreme competitiveness and egotism.

Mental Health and Heredity

Whenever some type of illness occurs and the individual cannot determine its nature, he or she may imagine that the affliction has been inherited. This situation appears to be particularly true of emotional illness, which has a tradition of being the least understood and, therefore, the most bewildering of all illnesses. The "logic" which has surrounded mental illness went something like this: If a person appeared happy and was materially successful, he must have inherited positive mental characteristics; if he seemed disturbed or confused and was not productive, he had inherited negative qualities and was emotionally ill.[42] Since it has only been during recent decades that medical strides have been made in the successful treatment of various types of mental illness, this social stigma still remains to a much greater degree than it should, and as a result many emotionally disturbed individuals continue to believe that they are doomed due to inheritance.

It is of the utmost importance that today's students develop an enlightened attitude toward heredity and mental health. It is vital that they understand that the study of genetics, as it affects inheritance, is a very new field of inquiry, which has developed primarily during the present century. In addition, only during the past two decades have there been concentrated research efforts to comprehend the molecular chemistry of genes, which determines the human genetic code. The significance of the genetic code is that it provides information about many aspects of human heredity. Even though some behavioral scientists continue to disagree over which is the more significant factor influencing human development, inheritance or environmental surroundings, current evidence strongly suggests that no one should entertain undue anxiety concerning heredity and mental health. This evidence indicates that one's environment is much more significant in the development of positive or negative emotional characteristics.[43]

The development and maintenance of good mental health is largely dependent upon an individual's development of positive attitudes toward himself and other people. However, these attitudes are not developed without learning processes. Students must understand that such values and attitudes will, to a large extent, determine whether they live happy and fulfilling lives, or whether their lives will be characterized by uncertainty, fear, suspicion, and anxiety—or, in reality, poor mental health.

TEACHING ABOUT NEUROTIC BEHAVIOR PATTERNS

Students must be aware that there are many thousands of individuals who suffer in varying degrees from mental difficulties which reflect neurotic symptoms. Such emotional problems include the inability to concentrate on specific tasks, such as reading or writing, irritability, unsociability, insomnia, extreme sensitivity, as well as milder forms of paranoia and depression. In addition to the symptoms of chronic anxiety from which anyone may suffer at times, there are many persons who possess particular types of symptoms, such as hysteria, temporary paralysis, sporadic blindness, an inability to communicate orally, along with other afflictions which would appear to be physical rather than mental in nature. Furthermore, there are numerous compulsive individuals who complain of continual doubts, are unable to make decisions, possess fears highly out of proportion to career or personal situations, display an inability to refrain from repetitive actions, such as making "certain" the doors are locked or committing crimes.[44]

Any human behavior patterns which possess these characteristics are termed neurotic. Students should understand that a neurosis, or psychoneurosis, is an illness resulting from inappropriate attempts to relieve mental tensions. Neurotic individuals express what are known to psychologists as "wish tensions" in disguised rather than in direct form, utilize similar reaction patterns repeatedly, and employ object displacement.

It is extremely vital, however, that students be able to distinguish between neurotic behavior—which, in general terms, is the manner in which all individuals get rid of their excess wish or desire energy in various disguised forms—and an actual neurosis—which is a form of mental illness characterized by too much neurotic behavior. By way of explanation, normal behavior reflects the efficient use of human energy, in a manner which is appropriate to the immediate circumstances, in order to satisfy easily recognized tensions by the demonstration of effective behavior toward the proper objects in the surrounding environment. In contrast, it must be emphasized that neurotic behavior patterns reflect a highly inappropriate waste of energy in an attempt to satisfy these tensions. Obviously, when demonstrated in moderation, much neurotic behavior is harmless, socially acceptable, and considered "normal." Only when such behavior becomes extreme and, therefore, harmful to the individual and potentially harmful to others, is it referred to as a neurosis.

The fact that a certain amount of human energy finds expression in neurotic behavior patterns most certainly does not always equal a neurosis. For instance, individuals who suffer from such functional disorders as chronic upset stomachs and headaches are not necessarily neurotics if they are able to fulfill their daily responsibilities effectively. Only when a high level of mental stress, resulting from the struggle between one's instincts and other forces of the mind, consumes so much energy that the individual feels bad or depressed for long periods, or is unable to achieve his or her potential in personality development or career responsibilities, is the individual suffering from a true neurosis. It must be continually emphasized to students that this distinction is the major difference between neurotic behavior and an actual neurosis as defined in clinical terms. A true neurosis is accompanied by a lessening of efficiency and a reduction or complete cessation of emotional growth.[45] Neurosis, therefore, may be defined as a desperate but unsuccessful attempt by the individual to satisfy basic needs. This point of view differs significantly from Freudian theory, as noted above, which hypothesized that neurotic behavior was an attempt on the part of the individual to satisfy unfulfilled needs, but failed to distinguish between legitimate needs and illegitimate needs. Regardless of which theoretical viewpoint one tends to follow, it is clear that the satisfaction of neurotic needs leads to a loss of capacity for the promotion of normal mental development.

PSYCHOSIS, PSYCHOTHERAPY, AND BEHAVIOR THERAPY

As secondary students are very much aware, most individuals are sufficiently in control of their neurotic tendencies so that most of their mental energy can be applied to positive purposes. In the case of these individuals, their emotional growth develops along normal patterns. Similarly, however, most secondary students have had an opportunity either to observe or to hear descriptions of individuals whose extreme neurotic characteristics have resulted in some form of what is commonly termed a "mental breakdown." When such a mental condition results in strange, abnormal forms of behavior, such behavior is termed a psychosis. In short, a psychotic is one who has lost control of his mental processes. It is most significant that students understand that *psychosis* is a medical term and refers to the loss (either temporary or long-term) of mental control, while *insanity* is a legal term which refers to the patient's inability to judge right from wrong in either a social or a legal sense.[46]

Psychosis

For purposes of classroom discussion of the phenomenon of psychosis, three major groups of psychosis may be identified: schizophrenic, organic, and depressive.

Schizophrenia

Schizophrenias are, in most instances, characterized by a personality split, partial or complete, between what actually happens to the individual and how he feels about it, with the result that the individual's feelings have little or no connection with real happenings or events. Such individuals are more interested in what might be defined as their daydreams than in what is actually taking place around them; their emotions depend more upon what goes on inside their minds than upon what happens outside.[47] At this point in any discussion of schizophrenic behavior, however, the instructor must make certain that students understand that daydreaming in moderation reflects normal behavior, that everyone daydreams, and that it is good for one's mental health. It is only when daydreaming nearly totally replaces reality that an individual possesses symptoms of schizophrenia. Schizophrenia, as a form of psychosis, represents an exaggerated example of the principle that people feel and act in accordance with their inner images rather than in accordance with reality. In summary, schizophrenics are characterized by the splitting of feelings from actual events and, in later stages of mental deterioration, the splitting of the mind into small segments which appear to act independently of one another.

Additionally, students should be aware that schizophrenics may be classified in four major categories. Furthermore, a particular individual may reflect each of these four types simultaneously, separately, or only one type of schizophrenic behavior throughout his or her entire illness. The first is a relatively simple type, characterized by the inability to become emotionally attached to anyone or anything. Thus, the individual wanders from place to place and from person to person. For instance, many vagabonds and prostitutes, who are constantly changing locations and companions, might be classified as simple schizophrenics. Obviously, this does not imply that everyone who changes vocations and human acquaintances with great frequency suffers from this disease. Only on an individual basis can clinical diagnosis determine whether there is a true lack of emotional attachment in an individual's life-style.

The second type of schizophrenia is known as the paranoid schizophrenic and is defined as a mental illness which is characterized by distorted thinking. In most instances, twisted thoughts become evident when the person has delusions about someone trying to harm him or that there is some type of conspiracy being directed against him. Additional characteristics of paranoia are that the individual reflects thoughts into imagined voices and visions, has a strong tendency to distort facts in order to justify his or her ideas, and possesses a general feeling of mistrust and suspicion toward others, and, in particular, those who are attempting to help the individual who is suffering.[48]

A third type of schizophrenia is referred to as catatonic. An individual suffering from this form of schizophrenia reflects a stoppage of almost all muscular movements and abrupt physical changes in muscular behavior, and is prone to committing acts of impulsive violence. A fourth form of this disease is termed hebephrenic. An individual suffering from this variety of schizophrenia behaves in a most unusual fashion and continually expresses many extremes, though oftentimes with sexual or ultrareligious overtones.[49]

It must further be emphasized to students that there are many psychotic individuals who, in all probability, would be cognizant of reality and know right from wrong. Similarly, there are individuals who reveal many of the symptoms of schizophrenia but should be treated by other means than psychotherapy.

Organic Psychosis

Anything which causes structural or chemical alterations in the human brain may result in what is known in medical terms as an organic psychosis. Among the physical afflictions which may result in such change are brain infections resulting from certain diseases, such as syphilis, meningitis, and tuberculosis. In addition there are other bodily infections, such as pneumonia, blood poisoning, and malaria, which are extremely infectious and result in high temperatures. Excessive use of alcohol and drug abuse may also weaken the brain structure and trigger psychotic symptoms, such as delirious behavior.[50]

Depression Psychosis

It is often difficult to distinguish between an individual who suffers from some type of schizophrenia and a particular form of depression psychosis. Perhaps the most significant point for students to remember when referring to such mental illnesses is that it is not the particular actions of the person that are of most significance, but rather the manner in which the individual carries out specific actions. For instance, an individual suffering from a severe depression may be highly disturbed by ideas of being personally persecuted, just as a person suffering from paranoid schizophrenia is characterized by severe conditions of depression.[51] However, students must understand that it is most difficult, if not impossible, for an untrained person to distinguish between the symptoms of a schizophrenic and the depressed feelings of a depressive. Such diagnosis requires years of clinical experience.

One national authority suggests that depressions should be classified into three major categories: (1) endogenous depressions, (2) reactive depressions, and (3) neurotic depressions.[52]

Endogenous Depressions. The term *endogenous* means "internally generated."[53] Such depressions develop when the brain and nervous system become disoriented in some manner and cannot function normally. The cause of such disorganization is commonly the result of some form of chemical imbalance within the nervous system. Psychiatrists might refer to this type of depression as an organic or physical disturbance negatively influencing the human nervous function.

It is vital that discussions regarding depression take into account some of the problems confronting people which may result in an illness. In the case of endogenous depressions, students should understand that a wide range of events might result in such a depression. Among the causes of endogenous depressions are forms of psychosis, such as schizophrenia, physical body infections, glandular disorders, serious accidents or injuries, surgery, excessive alcoholic consumption, drug abuse, childbirth, aging, changes in body structure, physical or mental fatigue, and menopause, or change of life, in both males and females.

Reactive Depressions. A major characteristic of the reactive type of depression is that the individual's attitudes are triggered by a sense of loss.[54] For instance, the person feels that permanence has been destroyed, resulting in the loss of security and the means of survival, particularly, economic survival. The feeling of loss, whether actual or imagined, appears so great to the individual that he or she is overwhelmed by grief. This extreme feeling of grief is known as a reactive depression. Reactive depressions may result from loss of relatives or friends through death; economic loss, such as losing one's job; situational changes like moving from place to place, divorce, or retirement. In addition, a prolonged period of loneliness or alienation from society may cause such depressions.

Neurotic Depressions. The neurotic type of depression is caused by the neurotic personality of the individual, the symptoms of which were discussed above.[55] Neurotic individuals are characterized by serious difficulties in the maintenance of stability. In effect, they are unable to tolerate the mental stresses found in day-to-day living. Rather than developing emotional strength by overcoming normal obstacles, their emotional capabilities are weakened because they waste so much mental energy on relatively minor situations. This process, if continued, eventually leads to emotional exhaustion, which commonly results in a prolonged period of neurotic depression.

In addition to being able to identify the particular reasons why some people become depressed, students should comprehend three essential factors which may be applied to all types of human depression: the intensity of the depression, the duration of the depression, and the quality of the depression.[56]

The intensity of a depression varies. It may be mild, moderate, or severe. Generally speaking, mild depression, even though distressing, can be overcome within a short time. Moderate and severe depressions are nearly universally classified as serious and, therefore, should be treated medically. The time-span or duration of a depression may be acute, recurrent, or chronic. An acute depression, for example, may appear rapidly but may last only a week or so and clear up without medical treatment. On the other hand, an acute depression may last for months or years even when being treated professionally. A recurrent depression can be defined as an acute depression that reappears at different intervals, with normal periods (referred to as "remissions") in between each occurrence. A chronic depression develops more rapidly and remains for an indefinite time, up to two or more years, with eventual periods of remission. The quality of a depression can be retarded where the person's physical and mental functions become slower, or it can attain an agitated state during which the person exhibits general nervous behavior.

It must be emphasized that many individuals, regardless of socioeconomic status, are susceptible to the development of severe or acute depressions throughout their lifetimes. Furthermore, the evidence is overwhelming that recovery to a stable mental level is dependent upon both medical treatment and a release from the circumstances, be they personal, social, or economic, which have produced the high level of emotional stress.

Psychotherapy and Mental Health

During the past few years, the term *psychotherapy* has become very popular, and undoubtedly it is a familiar word to many secondary students. In general, psychotherapy is the process through which an individual learns (1) how to examine his or her own values and attitudes, needs, decisions, and behavior patterns in relation to the values, needs, and behavior traits of those around him; (2) how to comprehend his values and behavior in order to resolve anxieties, doubts, fears, and conflicts; and (3) how to use such understanding to develop a happier and more successful life.[57] In essence, the psychotherapeutic technique for achieving these results consists of methods employed by psychiatrists, psychologists, and other behavioral scientists to influence the feelings, thinking processes, and behavior of individuals who are emotionally disturbed. When discussing this medical technique, it is important for students to understand that professional psychotherapy must be objective at all times. No form of dogmatic beliefs or personal bias should be involved. The basic concerns are the needs and anxieties of the patient so that his emotional disturbances may be overcome. Effective psychotherapy, therefore, requires professional and, in some instances, long-term treatment.

Behavior Therapy for Mental Health

This form of treatment consists of reeducating for a more successful life through a conditioning process. Such therapy can educate the chronically disturbed individual to perform his daily tasks with less anxiety and more incentive and optimism.[58]

Behavior therapy utilizes learning techniques and the principles of conditioning to instruct the individual how to modify and redirect negative personal behavior, values, and attitudes. For instance, it teaches him how to reduce tension, fear, and anger, and to replace such behavior with feelings of tranquility and relaxation. The ultimate objective of behavior therapy is to do away with the negative and rigid structural patterns that characterize the lives of many individuals, and to facilitate a new attitude and approach toward everyday living both in the personal and vocational realms.

Perhaps the primary goal of discussions concerning mental health in social studies is to promote the awareness among students that human problems involving mental or emotional health are constantly being examined in a much more "open" atmosphere than in the immediate past. The medical profession, educational agencies, and private employers have come to recognize that various types of mental illness, from moderate to acute forms, may strike anyone at any time. In addition, it is now widely accepted that such illness necessitates professional treatment, as do strictly physical afflictions. Thus, there need not be any fear or concealment whatsoever about admitting an emotional problem, seeking medical treatment, or discussing the wide range of mental afflictions to which we are all susceptible.

Assumptions for Student Inquiry

1. During recent decades, due to the fact that a greater proportion of the nation's population is suffering from various types of emotional disturbance, public attention has been directed more and more toward the area of mental health.
2. The proportion of our population which presently suffers from some form of mental illness is no greater now than at any time during the past. Rather, the topic of mental health is receiving more public concern because, as nations develop and mature, all aspects of the societal condition receive more widespread and positive attention.
3. The increase in mental illness nationally is due primarily to the increased stress which confronts individuals as they attempt to function productively in both their personal lives and their career pursuits in a technologically advanced, highly urbanized society.
4. In the United States, individuals residing in rural areas and smaller communities have proportionately fewer mental health problems than people living in large cities.
5. A much smaller proportion of the populations in less-developed countries suffer from extreme forms of mental illness than in technologically advanced, highly urbanized nations.
6. There is a positive correlation between technological and scientific advancement and an increase in the proportion of the population afflicted by symptoms of mental illness.
7. Most of the physical illnesses that afflict the people in this nation appear to be related to mental or emotional problems and stress.
8. The more intelligent the individual, the more potential dangers or pitfalls he or she can visualize in any given situation. As a result, highly intelligent individuals are more prone to develop the anxieties, fears, and suspicions that characterize poor emotional health and, therefore, are more susceptible to developing extreme forms of mental illness than are people of less innate intelligence.
9. At various times in their lives, all people suffer from some form of emotional disturbance that possesses the symptoms of mental illness.
10. The high rate of emotional disturbance and mental illness that characterizes the United States is largely due to the fact that the American educational system has not provided an adequate opportunity for individuals to learn how to deal successfully with the emotional stress of day-to-day living.
11. Since social interaction and individual competition, on both a personal and a career basis, will continue to become more complex during future decades in the United States, it is absolutely vital that the educational system devote a significant portion of its formal program to instruction in the area of mental health.
12. There is little that behavioral scientists, psychiatrists, or psychologists can contribute to the treatment and cure of mental illness, since the most significant determinant of an individual's emotional traits and emotional behavior is inheritance.
13. The great strides that behavioral scientists have made in the treatment and cure of extreme forms of mental illness would indicate that most forms of mental disease are not inherited, but rather are developed by the individual through his day-to-day living.

14. The basic factor influencing the individual's development of either positive or negative mental health is the social environment in which he lives and works.
15. If more individuals who are afflicted with minor emotional disturbances would acquire immediate professional consultation and treatment, many could be saved from developing extremely serious forms of mental illness.

ABORTION, EUTHANASIA, AND GENETIC MANIPULATION

Abortion, euthanasia, and genetic manipulation will each have a major effect upon human life during the remainder of the present century. Like the topics already discussed, all three are highly controversial on a political, religious, and cultural basis, and there is a great diversity of professional and social opinion, values, and attitudes in connection with each. Nevertheless, they will continue to gain significance in classroom discussions concerning the ever-changing human condition in technologically advanced societies.

The Abortion Question

The constantly changing value system of technologically advanced societies such as the United States was reflected in the Supreme Court's 1973 decision that "the Fourteenth Amendment's concept of personal liberty and restrictions upon state action" guarantees a privacy right that includes "a woman's decision whether or not to terminate her pregnancy."[59] However, the evolutionary rather than revolutionary nature of social change in an advanced society continues to be witnessed with regard to this social issue since the Court handed down its opinion.

In a democratic society, "laying down the law" is an expedient of last resort. This is especially true when a controversial issue is closely connected with conscience, and where large religious segments of society possess divergent but sincerely held views concerning the interpretation of what constitutes "right" conduct. Specifically, at the time of this writing, the Catholic hierarchy in the United States appears committed to overturning the Court's 1973 decision. Obviously, the legalities involved in reversing this decision could result in decades of unwanted and unprecedented religious antagonism.

The major principles for student comprehension, however, are the arguments of the opposing forces involved in this highly controversial issue, the processes by which attempts are made to resolve the question, and how changes in social values and attitudes evolve in a modern democratic society.

The highly charged nature of the abortion problem is exemplified by the argument of a proposed constitutional amendment forbidding abortion which has been launched by the Roman Catholic hierarchy. By striving to legalize the dictum that a human person exists at the moment of conception—which is one of the basic questions in the entire abortion debate—the Roman Catholic hierarchy has promoted a direct confrontation not only with the Supreme Court, but also with a large segment of Protestantism and Judaism. However, in a democratic society, when any religious denomination, regardless of how powerful (and since they comprise nearly a fifth of the American population, Roman Catholics are powerful), demands that private doctrine be translated into public law, not only is the religious structure strained, but the entire framework of mutual toleration in the nation is in serious danger. The ferocity of the charges made by Roman Catholicism against the defenders of legal abortion are stated in terms of "murder," "Nazi genocide," and so on, and are similar to the charges by elements of organized Christianity against the proponents of euthanasia, which are described below.

As with so many controversial social issues, students must understand that the national confrontation over the question of legal abortion revolves around religious tenets which can never be definitely resolved to the satisfaction of all concerned. For instance, the official Catholic position that the fertilized ovum is in actuality a human being is challenged by supporters of abortion as "metaphysical speculation."[60] Significantly, the Supreme Court refused to apply any theory as to "when life begins," stating that "when those trained in the respective disciplines of medicine, philosophy, and theology are unable to arrive at any consensus, the judiciary at this point in the development of man's knowledge is not in a position to speculate as to the answer."[61]

A central question for discussion, obviously, is whether any religious, political, or other interest group possesses the right to impose its moral views on other citizens who do not agree with those views and constitute a majority of the population. A related question, however, would be what restraints should be placed on the power of the majority to impose moral judgments, regardless of whether the issue involves sexual behavior, drug use, or abortion. Indeed, if there are no limits to the legal power of the majority, the result is a totalitarian political system. A major premise for student investigation is that in a democratic society, views on morality cannot be imposed by state dictum. Societal maturation may prove one value system right and another value system wrong, which is the major reason why American society has chosen to place limits upon the power of the state to encroach upon private moral choices. As our society has evolved, it has refrained, in most instances, from intruding too directly on decisions that are deeply personal, and it does not legally forbid everything that the majority considers objectionable.

Although abortion is a social issue around which much controversy will continue to revolve, improved family-planning procedures and birth-control techniques will contribute significantly to a reduction in unwanted pregnancies. Nevertheless, serious debate will probably continue regarding abortions of the therapeutic variety, or in cases where the health or life of the mother is endangered by childbirth.

Euthanasia

The term *euthanasia* is derived from the Greek word meaning "a good, or peaceful, death."[62] Like abortion, euthanasia has received ever-increasing support, particularly during the last two decades, and its proponents demand profound changes in our individual, social, and moral attitudes toward death.

As a framework for the discussion of euthanasia in social education, it should be emphasized that two contemporary developments have resulted in forcing the subject of euthanasia to the forefront of social morality and ethics in modern societies. First, advanced technology has reached the level whereby the medical profession possesses a much wider range of choices between life and death. Second is the ever-increasing demands of the individual to maintain and exercise his rights over matters affecting his mental health, physical health, and his right to live or die.

With regard to the former, in technologically advanced societies, mere biological existence can be prolonged indefinitely by artificial life-supporting mechanisms. Sophisticated apparatus, new drugs, and the artificial transplantation of vital organs can give a new lease on life to persons who, in many instances, would rather die. From the standpoint of human rights, the depressing evidence concerning needless human suffering continues to prompt the idea that people, like animals, have the legal and moral right to a merciful death, or euthanasia.

Like abortion, the concept of legalizing the right to a merciful death has raised many significant moral, social, legal, and medical questions. The proposals to legalize voluntary euthanasia, under stringent conditions, have resulted in considerable criticism from organized Christianity.[63] This is not surprising, since the sacredness of human life and personality is a fundamental tenet of the Christian faith. A basic concept for student awareness is that much of the criticism of euthanasia from organized religion, as well as other segments of society, involves both the relativity of the term and the negative precedent that legalized euthanasia could set for humanity.

Euthanasia, or mercy killing, is an idea that conjures up nearly as much fear as death itself among many. Indeed, it is one thing to translate the Greek word into "the good death"; it is another to be specific about such a benign term.[64] Such questions arise as: Is it something you do to yourself: suicide? Is it something others do to you: murder? Could it be used as an excuse for genocide: the mass killing of the innocent, young or old, who happen to be a "political," "economic," or "racial" burden on a particular society? The racial theories and mass extermination practices of the Nazi period in Germany continue to haunt the Western world, and reinforce the fear of any legislation that could result in a repetition of this tragic era in contemporary history.

In its literal connotation, euthanasia, in the voluntary sense, reflects none of these social tragedies. Its legal and moral interpretation means that any individual who is incurably sick or miserably senile, whose condition is hopeless, and who desires to die, should be enabled to do so; and that he should be enabled to do so without his incurring, or his family incurring, or those who provide or administer the means of death incurring, any legal penalty or moral stigma whatsoever.

It is important for students to realize that the concept of euthanasia, like most contemporary controversial social themes, has been evolving for a long period.[65] Nevertheless, in the United States, as in all societies, the power structures of both state and church have constantly rejected legislation deemed likely to result in the individual right of choice involving matters of life and death. The only way that governing establishments, until recent years, have been able to maintain their sovereignty in such matters has been to keep their inhabitants within the framework of legal and religious patterns that may have served society well at one time, but have now, largely as a result of technological advances, ceased to be useful to humanity. Throughout any discussion of euthanasia, it should continually be stressed that even though we are in many respects a violent society, reacting violently to various forms of official doctrine or human prejudice, we are also a nation in which capital punishment for major crimes is becoming increasingly rare.

Eugenics

Each generation of mankind is confronted with the awesome responsibility of having to make certain decisions concerning the quantity and quality (both genetic and cultural) of future generations. Due mainly to the concern for its increasing population in relation to the ability of the natural environment to provide the resources for a continuing high quality of life, the United States has discarded its policy of encouraging continued population growth and has adopted a policy aimed at achieving a zero rate of population growth by voluntary means. A vital principle for student understanding is that the particular policy that a society adopts with respect to population size and growth rate will have genetic as well as environmental consequences.[66]

Human populations adapt to their environments genetically as well as culturally. By creating a highly technological nation, the United States has produced a society in which a significant and ever-increasing proportion of its citizens will not be able to contribute to its growth or maintenance because of genetic limitations of their intellect. The technologically advanced societies throughout the world offer their citizens a wide range of opportunities for self-realization and advancement, but are witnessing the fact that a growing proportion of their populations are incapable of taking advantage of the varied opportunities open to them.

American society, if it takes its responsibility to future generations seriously, will have to do more than control the size of its population in relation to the environment. American society will have to take steps to insure that individuals yet unborn will have the best genetic and environmental heritage possible to enable them to meet the challenges of the environment and to take advantage of the opportunities for self-fulfillment made available by a modern society.[67]

The question of genetic quality cannot be ignored for long by American society. For instance, the technologically based, computer-age sociocultural environment continually being created in the United States has placed a premium on individual possession of high intelligence and intellect. Our advanced society requires individuals with high levels of intelligence and creativity to help it make the appropriate social and technological adjustments in order to culturally adapt to its rapidly changing environment. Also, individuals require high intelligence and creativity in order that they, as individuals, can successfully deal with the challenges of both the natural and cultural environment and take advantage of the opportunities for self-fulfillment present in our advanced society.

Significantly, the proportion of the American population that already is genetically handicapped—that suffers a restriction of liberty or competence as a result of their genetic makeup—is not small. Therefore, the genetic component of the human population-environment equation must be taken into account as we attempt to establish a natural and cultural environment that has a high degree of sociological stability and maximizes the number of opportunities for self-fulfillment available to each individual human being.[68]

Society in the United States has developed advanced medical technology which enables many individuals with severe genetic defects to survive to adulthood. Many of these individuals can and do reproduce, passing their harmful genes on to the next generation and, thereby, increasing the frequency of these genes in the total population. Presently, there is no valid evidence that heredity counseling decreases the probability that these individuals will have children. Indeed, the life-styles of these individuals in terms of reproduction is creating a larger and larger genetic burden for future generations of Americans to bear.

The overall net effect of current American life-styles in reproduction appears to be slightly dysgenic—to be favoring an increase in harmful genes which will genetically handicap a larger proportion of the next generation of Americans. American life-styles in reproduction are, in part, a function of the population policy of the United States.[69]

Genetic Implications of Compulsory Population Control

At this point, students might be asked to suggest some of the possible genetic consequences if a nation like the United States had to resort to mutual coercion, or employ compulsory methods of population control, to control the natural rate of population increase.

There are a number of methods through which compulsory population control can be achieved. In a democratic society like the United States, mutual coercion could be institutionalized to insure that couples who would otherwise be reproductively irresponsible are restricted to producing only two children. Compulsory abortion and/or sterilization could be employed to guarantee that no woman has more children than she has a right to under the established rules.[70]

A democratic society forced to employ mutual coercion to achieve zero population growth would probably assign everyone the right to have exactly two children. Because of the fact that some individuals would have only one child or would not reproduce at all, it would be necessary to assign these births needed to achieve replacement level to other individuals within the population. The result would probably be genetic deterioration even if the natural environment remained constant.[71] However, if the environment were changing (and an ever-changing environment is a definite constant), the population would become even more genetically ill-adapted because those individuals in the society that are best adapted to changing environments and new environments would not be passing on more genes to the next generation, on a per person basis, than those individuals less well adapted.

What kinds of eugenics programs could be designed for a democratic society where mutual coercion is institutionalized to insure that couples who would otherwise be irresponsible are restricted to having two children?

One compulsory population-control program that has eugenic implications would be to grant marketable licenses to have children to women in whatever number necessary to insure replacement of the population.[72] If equality of opportunity were the norm, those individuals with genetic makeups that enable them to succeed (high intelligence, personality, etc.) would be successful in reaching the upper echelons of society and would be in the position of being able to purchase certificates from individuals who were less successful because of their genetic limitations. The marketable-baby-license approach would probably bring about a better genetic adaptation between a population and its environment.

An additional compulsory population program which a society might adopt would be that of granting each individual the right to have two children, and of assigning the childbearing rights of those individuals unable or unwilling to have two children to other individuals, based upon their performance in one or more contests (competitions involving mental ability, personality, sports, music, arts, literature, business, etc.).

A society might go even further and employ a simple eugenic test—the examination of the first two children in order to assure that neither one was physically or mentally below the average—which a couple must pass before being eligible to have additional children.[73]

The programs designed to bring about a eugenic distribution of births that have been discussed above may prove to be incapable of doing much more than counteracting the input of harmful mutations. In order to significantly reduce the proportion of the population that is genetically handicapped, a society might have to require that each couple pass certain eugenic tests before being allowed to become the genetic parents of any children. If one or both of the prospective genetic parents fail the eugenic tests, the couple could still be allowed to have children via artificial insemination and/or artificial inovulation, utilizing human sperm and eggs selected on the basis of genetic quality. Such an approach would enable society to maintain the right of couples to have at least two children while improving the genetic birthright of future generations at the same time.

Successful control of the genetic quality of human populations by society may require restrictions on the right of individual human beings to reproduce. The right of individuals to have as many children as they desire must be considered in relation to the right of individuals yet unborn to be free from genetic handicaps and to be able to live in a high-quality environment.[74] The short-term gain in individual freedom attained in a society that grants everyone the right to reproduce, and to have as many children as they want, can be more than offset by the long-term loss in individual freedom by individuals yet unborn who, as a consequence, are genetically handicapped and are forced to live in an environment that has deteriorated due to the pressure of human numbers.[75]

Assumptions for Student Inquiry

1. In a democratic society like the United States, the legal right to an abortion should, in every instance, be a personal decision.
2. The right to an abortion should not be a personal decision alone since another human being comes into existence at the moment of conception.
3. If abortion is legalized on a universal basis, it will be a first significant step toward the legalized genocide of older people, ill people, and people considered to be "undesirable" for religious, social, political, or other reasons by the majority of society.
4. No religious, political, or other segment of society has the right to impose its beliefs concerning abortion on other elements of society.
5. Every individual should possess the right to die when he or she desires to cease living for whatever reason.
6. It should not be considered the moral duty of the medical profession to prevent death when there is no medical hope for the individual other than that of prolonging life.
7. If euthanasia, or mercy killing, becomes a common practice, there is the constant danger that it could be employed by governments for the purpose of destroying their political enemies, minority groups, or other segments of society.
8. It is absolutely vital in a democratic society that euthanasia must remain on a voluntary basis.
9. The government of a democratic society cannot restrict the number of children that a couple may produce, even if the parents possess severe genetic defects.
10. If the population of the United States is to maintain the level of technical and intellectual competence necessary to keep the nation in its present position of international preeminence, it will become necessary to impose strict monetary penalties or require the sterilization of persons with genetic defects.

PROBLEMS OF LEISURE, AGING, AND DEATH

The Concept of Leisure

The interrelationships between an individual's work and his or her leisure time often determine the overall quality of life in a society. In a technological nation which is rapidly becoming a posttechnological society, such as the United States, increasing affluence produces more leisure time for members of the labor force. With the further influence of economic affluence and automation and the resultant decrease in necessary labor time, American society will have to reexamine its traditional conception of work as well as the meaning of leisure. Ultimately, it may be discovered not only that play is hard work, but that, pursued as an end in itself, it can be every bit as demanding as work. This situation represents one of those paradoxes that only a posttechnological society could encounter.

Many of today's secondary students will retire (either voluntarily or by coercion) from their careers or professions between the ages of forty and fifty. Indeed, by 1985 the problems of today's elderly are going to be the problems of the middle-aged. Furthermore, by the decade of the 1980s, a three- or four-day work-week—almost halved since 1900—means that even the young will be marginally retired.[76]

For purposes of classroom discussion, the concept of leisure can be presented around several themes for student analysis. First, the cause of increased leisure time in an advanced society might be examined. Students should comprehend that leisure is related directly to advances in scientific and industrial technology which result in work efficiency. The progress made in work efficiency is reflected immediately in leisure. Technological advancement means increased production, which, in turn, usually results in a higher living standard. Thus, the majority of the population in modern societies have shorter working hours, more leisure, and also more money to spend. The impact of automation must also be introduced. Specifically, the same tremendous scientific and technological strides which produced thermonuclear energy and space exploration have also developed automation in all economic sectors, which has resulted in a further reduction in the work-week, which implies social problems as well as potentials for social progress. In addition, continued advances in medical technology have vastly increased both the amount and significance of leisure time. While automation compresses the actual period of gainful employment, modern medical techniques, together with better practices in health care and sanitation, help prolong the human life span, which, obviously, results in more years for leisure activity.[77]

With the advancements in science and industrial technology, and their concomitants of automation and modern medicine, leisure may indeed become the center of our advanced culture. This does not imply the end of work, however. Automation, for instance, can liberate the worker from dull, repetitive, monotonous, and often hazardous types of labor in polluted environments, but it cannot contribute significantly to personal gratification. Similarly, higher living standards, greater productivity, and increased income resulting from technological sophistication and longer life expectancy through medical advancements most certainly will not, in themselves, insure feelings of greater individual purpose and dignity. It must be emphasized to students that these advancements, which are the products of a highly modernistic society, will necessitate a reassessment of human value systems, both for the individual and society, if they are to result in positive behavior patterns.

The Work Ethic and the Leisure Ethic

Social studies education will have many new tasks during future decades. It is doubtful whether any of its responsibilities are greater than that of educating for human freedom in its most literal sense. The social education program must prepare youth to accept and utilize positively many more years of leisure time, and more years of life expectancy as well. What is actually required is the development of a new type of citizen—an individual who possesses confidence in his or her own limitless potentials, a person who is not intimidated by the prospect of not actively pursuing a career after the age of forty-five, and an individual who comprehends that technology can produce an easier world but only mankind can produce a better one.

Most students are familiar with such traditional clichés as "Play is the work of children" and "Idle hands do the devil's work." Such statements constantly reinforced work as one of the most important human values. The value system associated with the work ethic must be adjusted to fit the leisure ethic. In American society, the work ethic is rapidly giving way to the new leisure ideal.[78] Today, and throughout the future, the educational system must place the quality of human life ahead of technological advancement. This adaptation of a new value system, which will provide individuals with lifelong self-respect and fulfillment based upon the productive use of leisure time, must now become a major objective of social education in modern societies. Today's student must be educated to view leisure, not as a vacation from work, but rather as a vocation in itself. For youth in the mid-1970s, the personal values that make life worth living must be found in leisure time. If this objective is not accomplished in the near future, the concept of leisure could become more of a societal tragedy than thermonuclear war.

Aging in American Society

With life expectancy continually increasing (currently over seventy years of age when averaging both male and female), and modern science predicting its immediate capability to extend life expectancy thirty additional years,[79] and, ultimately, to 150 years,[80] the study of gerontology, the science of aging, will gain ever-increasing significance for today's secondary school youth.

Perhaps the primary rationale for the consideration of aging in secondary education is, again, to attempt to promote a change in the traditional attitude regarding the concept of aging in our society on the part of today's student. Not only will youth be confronted individually with this issue during their later adult lives, but the society in which they live and function will continue to have a significantly larger proportion of "older" people, due to the continued decline in the birth rate and increased longevity.

As an organizational framework for considering the theme of aging in social education, it would seem that students must be aware that in the modern world, the roles and status of various groups in any given society, including the role and status of the aged, are very likely to be strongly influenced by the degree of modernization of that society. From nearly every standpoint, the United States is the most technologically advanced of all contemporary societies. The nation is Western in tradition since most of its citizens are descendants of immigrants from Europe.

Nearly all of these immigrants emerged from societies in which the Judeo-Christian tradition was dominant, and most of them were Protestants imbued with the work-ethic and its concomitant vaunted individualism. In such an individualistic society, these values were interpreted to mean that each person must earn his own way by his own efforts. Furthermore, failure was commonly considered to be the result of a lack of moral "fiber," incompetence, or inadequacy, and was viewed as degradation in the eyes of the community.[81] As a greater proportion of the population became further removed from the immigrant generation, as the frontier continued to expand westward, and as the Protestant ethic was gradually softened by the evolving realities of urban growth, many of these social values began to undergo gradual change. Nevertheless, many vestiges of these cultural values continue to remain in our society during the latter half of the twentieth century.

The United States has become a nation of high social mobility and rapid change. The nation has always been an open society with much intragenerational and intergenerational social mobility.[82] Such high mobility tends continually to blur the lines of social class and make particular social classes highly unstable. A result of individual social mobility is a high degree of social change in society at large. In such a social setting, many individuals achieve higher status by contributing new ideas, new inventions, and new skills, and this contributes to intergenerational mobility by making it possible for members of younger generations to enter newly created vocations. This situation, and the continued obsolescence of other modes of life, contributes to the ever-widening gap between the generations.[83]

The central questions for student analysis, therefore, revolve around such vital issues as: What does it mean to grow older in this type of dynamic society? At what age is an individual considered old? How do older people rate in comparison to younger age groups in such a technologically advanced, individualistic, ever-evolving, automated, and affluent society? Under what circumstances will cultural attitudes change in a society which values youthfulness and productivity?

By the year 2000, nearly 12 percent of the population of the United States, or an estimated 30 million people, will be at least sixty-five years old.[84] More significantly, however, from the standpoint of social stereotyping, many of these "older" people will not have been employed in any economic sector of the nation for twenty to twenty-five years previous, or since they were forty to forty-five years of age. What age group, then, will constitute the "aging"?

The "Graying" of America

In relation to previous discussions concerning the population dynamics of the United States, students should be made aware that one of the most dramatic effects of a sustained low birth rate will be what is presently being termed the "graying" of America.[85] A decreasing birth rate will result in a declining proportion of younger people and an increasing proportion of older people within the absolute population. For example, it should be pointed out that today (1975), youth under fifteen years of age represent about 30 percent of the nation's total population—nearly three times more than the portion of the population over the age of sixty-five (approximately 10 percent). When zero population growth is achieved, those under fifteen and those over sixty-five years will both account for 20 percent of the population if the average American life expectancy remains unchanged. However, if life expectancy increases a few years, as it undoubtedly will, the proportion of older people will be even larger. In essence, during the next half-century the number of people over sixty-five will at least double.[86]

The significance of this change in the age structure of the American population is that as the nation's median age moves upward from twenty-eight today to nearly thirty-eight during the middle of the twenty-first century, so will the average age of those who influence social trends and life-styles. Even now, older Americans are more likely to vote than younger people, and as this age group increases in numbers, it will also become a greater political force. Thus, there will be a tendency for the aging proportion of the population to become more powerful and influential.

Even though there is evidence that older people are more conservative than younger people, a brief review of our contemporary national development reveals that some of the most radical political ideas have been promoted by lobbies representing older people. Furthermore, students must understand that definitions of what is conservative change over time. For instance, medicare and social security, which constitute favorite issues of senior citizens, were once considered extremely radical proposals. In addition, both Sweden and Denmark have experienced a lower birth rate for several decades, which has resulted in an increase in the age level of the total population, but there have been no alterations in the basic liberal political, social, and economic policies of these nations.

Some experts on gerontology predict an "age backlash" in future decades—a period of political ferment in which older people will emerge as the dominant group advocating social change. In support of this premise, gerontologists point to trends already becoming evident in a few urban areas, where "gray panthers" have been organizing to demand better housing and transportation facilities, increased social security benefits, and improved medical care.[87]

On the basis of these observations, it would seem imperative that today's secondary school youth become familiar with as many of the political and social ramifications of aging as possible, since the concept of age might well become the next major frontier of behavioral research as our nation enters the stage of a posttechnological society.

The Study of Death

During the past half-decade, courses dealing with social and personal attitudes toward dying and death have become highly popular in colleges and universities throughout the nation. If past educational trends are any indication, fields of study which gain prominence in higher education will emerge in the precollegiate curricular structure within a short time span. With the increasing emphasis being placed upon the consideration of behavioral patterns in social studies, it appears inevitable that such a relevant phenomenon as death will constitute a significant topic for study in secondary education during the immediate future.

The primary emphasis of discussions concerning death that are designed for youth of secondary school age should probably involve the following three fundamental questions: Why is death viewed as such a negative event in our society? What happens after one dies? What does it "feel like" to experience dying?

Despite Christian tenets with reference to heaven and the beginning of an afterlife, death is viewed by most adults and youth as a tragedy. Indeed, it might be quite accurate to speculate that much of the fear and avoidance reactions with reference to old age in American society could be interpreted to be a psychological reaction to old age in terms of its implicit temporal connection with death.[88] Students are aware that the topic of death is a subject society avoids, not to be discussed or considered until it is forced upon us. Thus, death usually comes as a shock, and one is rarely mentally prepared for it. The fear of death, therefore, is a prevalent emotion.

The United States, as noted previously, is a highly materialistic, time-conscious, production-motivated society. In such a society, death is the only human event which results in a cessation of these activities. At this point, students should be encouraged to examine the premise that it is only in an advanced technological society, which has succeeded so well in postponing death, that death becomes so firmly associated with old age, with the result, as noted above, that aging is feared, resisted, and resented. When death intrudes itself into the consciousness of Americans, it comes in the nature of an unexpected and an unprepared for occurrence. Therefore, it is one of the relatively few occasions in the life-cycle which involves elaborate rites.[89]

To remove the emotion of fear from the dying process and death would appear to be a major objective of instruction about death. Students should be instilled with the concept of viewing death as a developmental task in the sense that an individual must learn to view his own death as the appropriate outcome of life. The goal would be to portray to youth that dying and death do not represent submission to blind fate. Rather, death represents the acceptance of life's conclusion in terms of its positive fulfillment.

Assumptions for Student Inquiry

1. Due to the rapid advancements being made in automation, in addition to the trends for a shortened work-week and earlier retirement age, leisure-time activities will

account for more than one-half of an individual's lifetime by the twenty-first century.

2. During the next few decades, the American educational system will have to place priority upon educating youth both to engage in productive leisure-time activities and to develop a positive value system toward the availability of large amounts of leisure time during their lives.

3. Continued strides in technology and automation will result in more rather than fewer lifetime career and vocational opportunities during future decades.

4. By the year 2000, and throughout the twenty-first century, American society will become middle-aged and older in its composition rather than youth-oriented as it is today.

5. As life expectancy increases and the birth rate continues to decline, social mores, life-styles, and political and economic legislation will become much more conservative in the United States since the majority of the population will be over thirty-five years of age by the year 2025.

6. During future decades, the fear of aging will be greatly diminished since society's attitudes toward older people and their vocational and social contributions will become much more positive than they are today.

7. By the year 2000, American medical technology will possess the ability to increase average life expectancy from slightly over seventy years, as it is today, to over one hundred years.

8. The subjects of dying and death must be included as systematic topics for discussion in the American educational system before society's negative attitude toward these subjects will be diminished significantly.

As the social studies curriculum places more emphasis upon individualized instruction, individual behavioral characteristics will also gain greater significance within the formal educational system. As a result, students will need to be provided more and more opportunity to examine both their own behavior patterns and those of other individuals. Such reflection should contribute greatly in helping students to clarify and define their own values and attitudinal systems as they prepare to enter adult life.

CHAPTER 6

Group Behavioral Patterns

URBANIZATION IN MODERN AMERICA

Currently, the population of the United States is approximately 213 million. Even if present demographic trends continue to reflect a decline in the birth rate (most population projections indicate only slight variations in the growth rate to the year 2000),[1] there will be between 265 and 280 million Americans by the year 2000. Where these 50 to 70 million additional citizens are to live will continue to be one of the foremost problems confronting demographers. Can American society provide them a place without disrupting the fabric of society or reducing its quality? Social critics have been proclaiming the crisis of the cities for decades. If social problems are related to population growth during the last fifty years, they are also connected with the phenomenal rate of urbanization of the last thirty years, and the suburbanization or suburban movement that began shortly thereafter.

The effects of rapid population growth are underscored by this characteristic of American demographic behavior of the last few decades: the tremendous urbanization and concentration of population in metropolitan areas. Today, some 74 percent of the American population reside in urban areas of 50,000 or more. Demographic projections indicate that during the remainder of the 1970s this urban proportion will increase by nearly 60 million people, an increase equivalent to some twenty cities the size of Los Angeles. Viewing this urban phenomenon from another perspective, 42 percent of our present population, or nearly 84 million people, live in thirty-three metropolitan areas of more than 1 million each.[2] Indeed, it has been projected that by 1990 three major megalopolitan areas will comprise over 65 percent of the nation's population.[3] Similar projections indicate that by the year 2000, more than 85 percent of the American population will be urban (living in cities of 50,000 or more).[4]

The United States is now in the era of the suburbs. During recent years practically all of the growth in metropolitan areas was in the suburban rings, including middle-class residential, upper-class residential, and commuter zones. Since 1960, for instance, the central-city areas of metropolitan regions have grown only by about 1 percent, while the suburban areas have increased by nearly 30 percent.[5] Furthermore, the population balance between central cities and the suburban rings has clearly shifted since 1960. At that time, suburban areas had slightly fewer people than the central cities. Since then, more than half the people in the nation's metropolitan areas live outside central cities, and every indication is that this fraction will increase well into the twenty-first century, regardless of speculation that vast federally subsidized housing projects in the central cities will result in a reverse migration from the suburban areas. The dynamics of our existing urban configurations have generated a momentum which is likely to produce more of the same in the future, unless a systematic effort is launched to create new opportunities for the approximately 60 million new Americans who will have to find homes within the next two and one-half decades.

The Urban Environment

Problems associated with the varying aspects of urban growth are among the most crucial domestic issues confronting the social studies curriculum. The basic social studies concepts of human respect and interdependence must be made more relevant to the pressing social needs existing in the nation's urban areas. Social studies teachers are directly responsible for instilling attitudes and values in adolescents that can contribute to the solution of these crucial problems. Indeed, in a society in which nearly 80 percent of the population will be living in cities over 50,000 in size by the end of the present decade, promoting an awareness of the urban problems in the United States nearly equals promoting an awareness of most of the societal issues currently confronting the nation.

Future Urban Trends

A significant principle for student understanding is that the physical characteristics of urbanization have produced radical changes in American social values and attitudes. It can be expected that the spatial segregation (the central city, the suburbs, and commuter zones) in metropolitan areas on the basis of race, ethnic origin, religious affiliation, and social class status will change very slowly, if at all, during the remainder of the century. If poverty can in fact be eliminated, segregated areas based on differentials of wealth will become less prominent without ever disappearing entirely. Furthermore, if social attitudes change, involuntary ghettos may be eliminated. For instance, new mass transit systems may provide the urban dweller of the future with a flexibility and a convenience unknown today, and may significantly shape the land-use patterns of tomorrow. The ability to predict future urban environmental trends is dependent, however, upon the ability to control the direction of social change in urban areas and in society at large.

The irregular and changing residential and commercial areas in metropolitan regions are characterized by shifting boundaries and the human conflict that such change generates, by the lack of genuine homogeneity within the ghettos themselves, by the presence of increasing numbers of minority-group members in nonsegregated areas, and by the denial of any official institutional support for their maintenance. The indefinite continuance of the involuntary ghetto in its present form thus seems highly unlikely in view of the pressures from various sources for greater equality in all areas of social life.

It is reasonable to assume that any objective classroom discussion of urban social and physical patterns will probably result in the following major conclusion on the part of students: voluntary residential segregation based upon race, religion, education, income, and personal affinities—exemplified by the suburbs of most American cities, by the persisting ethnic enclaves within central cities, and by economically homogeneous neighborhoods—will probably continue indefinitely. It should be emphasized that even in nations where housing is completely controlled by the government, urban residential areas continue to be differentiated in terms of particular valued social characteristics. [6]

Strategies for Presenting Urban Problems

If the instructional techniques in urban studies in the metropolitan areas have to be varied, then the instructional materials employed in these studies must be varied also. Obviously, there is an agglomeration of materials on urban living. However, most of these materials are nebulous, highly descriptive, and probably meaningless to most students living in the inner city. [7] Indeed, if teaching about urban life is to have genuine significance, it should be based upon the obvious and the substantial. Valid learning experiences for students in social studies classes will result from a consideration of the past as it has contributed to present-day life in the urban area.

Many of the issues that educators now refer to as "urban problems" or the "urban crisis" have characterized the American city for at least a century. A classroom environment in which students are directed to inquire into the past causes of present situations will make them much better equipped to comprehend the city as it exists today, and to understand what possible alternative solutions are needed to improve the human condition in urban areas.

To instruct students about the inner city in which they reside, or to describe the living conditions existing in the inner city to suburban, small-town, or rural students, by emphasizing the state of physical and human decadence and environmental deterioration, accomplishes little to promote valid understanding. A much more positive approach would be to point out the background of the forces that have contributed to the negative urban condition, namely, urban decay, racial conflict, substandard housing, drug abuse, alcoholism, crime, and so on. Furthermore, it is highly doubtful that introducing instructional units in urban behavioral problems will contribute much to the promotion of student inquiry into the relationship of urbanites to their physical and social environment.

Secondary students comprehend ideas and concepts best by relating to relevant and specific issues. What could be more concrete than understanding the problems that students in urban areas live, that they view about their home environment on television, that they hear discussed in their homes and at school among their classmates. [8] Students are bombarded through the mass media by racial conflicts, group dissent, and other happenings of a similar nature, but often teachers are hesitant to discuss such news items in their classrooms. Usually, it is in the central or inner city that these events are most common; therefore, a study of the human condition and the characteristics of disadvantaged youth in the inner city would be incomplete without discussing these events. Social studies teachers must attempt to stimulate youth to view firsthand the results of crowding many ethnic groups into a ghetto, the disparity in socioeconomic characteristics of the suburbanite and the ghetto resident, and the high density of blacks and other racial minorities in the inner city, as these phenomena are related to contemporary urban problems.[9]

The Urban Crisis as a Human Crisis

Some urbanologists frequently remark that the greatest threat to the future of mankind in global context, next to thermonuclear war, lies in "the problem of cities."[10] Statements of this type, however, mistake problems "in" the cities for problems "of" the cities. Obviously, poverty, unemployment, crime, racial discrimination, mental illness, alcoholism, drug addiction, and other crucial social problems are to be found in urban areas, but they should be presented as problems of society rather than problems of cities. These problems are much more visible in metropolitan areas because that is where the greatest density of the population is concentrated. Thus, these issues force themselves on the conscience of society.[11] Were the same human problems distributed throughout nations in isolated pockets, national attention would not be so forcefully directed to them.

For purposes of class discussions, social problems may be defined as recurrent events that involve sizable groups of people, that cause distress either to the people directly involved or to the members of the larger society, and that are believed to be subject to amelioration or prevention through a change in the organization of the society as a whole, or in some part of that society. Social problems exist if one or a combination of the following four basic situations occur:

1. There are relatively widespread violations of the majority social-behavior norms. Unemployment, poverty, crime, alcoholism, drug abuse, and racial discrimination are examples of group behavior patterns that characterize this category.
2. There exists a significant deviation from what is generally accepted as an attainable level of health. Physical and mental health problems that are considered either to result from man-controlled causes, such as venereal disease and occupational diseases, or to be receiving less than the optimum treatment or prevention commensurate with the present level of medical knowledge, are also considered social problems.
3. More financially solvent segments of society must meet the financial costs of care for other elements of society because the persons receiving the benefits cannot pay for them. Payment through taxation for unemployment benefits and welfare subsidies would also be included in this category.
4. Instances where society is failing to provide for the vocational, intellectual, and social fulfillment or potential of its members. Classified in this category would be

such things as the failure to attain educational levels commensurate with ability and widespread subjective feelings of worthlessness, boredom, or isolation.[12]

These could be considered as the individual and group social problems which are commonly termed "urban problems." They represent problems of people rather than problems of a physical environment. The basic questions for student inquiry involve the extent to which the urban physical environment is the cause (direct or indirect) of social problems, and what measures must be taken to improve the environmental quality of urban areas.

For purposes of concluding a discussion of urbanization, the instructor should continually emphasize the concept that as metropolitan communities in the United States become older and larger, differences in population characteristics between the central city and the outlying areas, as well as the changes in the economic base of suburbia itself, increase the apathy or indifference on the urban periphery to the problems of the urban center. The economic consequence resulting from urban subdivision is that many suburbanites gain their livelihood from the central city but pay taxes for property, education, and income only in the suburb, thus removing both financial and human resources from the central city, with its increasing problems of physical deterioration, unemployment, poverty, crime, mental illness, and racial conflict. It is little wonder that many urban planners strongly recommend the creation of more comprehensive political units based upon the new standard metropolitan area[13] rather than upon the central city and the politically autonomous suburban satellites.

The manner in which urban studies are present in the classroom atmosphere is highly significant if the ultimate educational objectives are to be achieved. A priority must be placed upon individual attention, so that students' values, attitudes, and abilities will be directed in positive directions to produce conscientious and responsible citizens. To achieve such results demands innovative, creative, open-minded instructors who can develop a classroom atmosphere conducive to the pursuance of improving the urban human condition.

Assumptions for Student Inquiry

1. By the year 2000, approximately 85 percent of the United States population will be residing in cities over 50,000 referred to as standard metropolitan areas.
2. By the year 2000, over 75 percent of the nation's population will be residing in three major urban areas referred to as "megalopoli": the eastern seaboard, the West Coast, and from the Gulf Coast to the Great Lakes region.
3. Future population movements in urban areas will result in the migration of many people from the suburbs back into the central city due to a combination of reasons, including extremely high property taxes in the suburbs, ever-increasing commuting distances, and availability of lower-cost rental housing and apartment complexes in the central city.
4. The increasing inner-city urban population will reside in large, federally subsidized, multi-unit apartment complexes, which will be largely self-contained, with medical,

recreational, shopping, and educational facilities. As a result, the single-family dwelling unit will have largely disappeared in the inner city by the year 2000.

5. The next metropolitan "slum" areas will be the suburbs, due to the migration back to the central cities financed by both private capital and ever-increasing federal financial support.

6. Due to rapidly increasing traffic congestion, private automobiles will be outlawed in the environs of the inner city by the end of the present century. All inner-city transportation will be public transportation.

7. The only solution to the urban crisis is to redistribute the city populations into metropolitan areas of between 50,000 and 100,000 in the sparsely inhabited regions of the country.

8. Due to the enormous scope of the nation's urban problems, any solutions will depend almost entirely upon the expenditure of federal funds.

9. The continuing period of urban growth in the United States has made it possible for individuals of lower socioeconomic status and members of minority groups to improve their social, economic, and political status.

10. If large metropolitan areas were fragmented and redistributed into smaller urban areas, much of the social and economic progress which minority groups and lower socioeconomic groups have achieved during the past century would be largely destroyed.

RACIAL-CULTURAL ASSIMILATION AND ETHNIC RELATIONS

For the remainder of the twentieth century and during the twenty-first century, the secondary social studies program will make an outstanding contribution to American social cohesiveness if it can achieve substantial progress toward the achievement of ethnic assimilation among the various segments of the nation's population. It would seem that for the educational system to emphasize integration among diverse ethnic groups in a locational or geographical context only will fall far short of achieving the ultimate goal of socializing the various cultural elements comprising American society. Indeed, minority-group peoples must be accepted in a psychological sense by the vast majority of the white population before the terms *civil rights* and *integration* will have any valid significance in a national sense. Thus, the social studies program must emphasize cultural assimilation in addition to locational integration. Specifically, this implies that social studies instructors must instill positive values, ideals, and respect, and strive to promote the appropriate mental set among students representing all racial groups. Only when acceptance of others is achieved in psychological terms can racial prejudice be eliminated and valid racial integration (assimilation) be achieved.

A most significant national objective for student awareness is that governmental policy in all advanced societies must promote a policy of minority-group integration. Such a policy is vital to the achievement of civil rights and, ultimately, to national security, since no nation can afford to risk substantial segments of its population—due to minority traits or traditions—to be outside the economic, political, and social mainstream of society. In the interest of national viability and national survival, therefore, every attempt must be made to strive toward the achievement of this objective.

Throughout the entire educational system the social studies curriculum has the primary responsibility, in relation to all other curricular areas, for developing the instructional strategies that will eventually achieve the objective of improving minority-group relations and instilling within American youth the necessary cross-cultural attitudes and values to achieve an integrated society.

Collective Behavior and Social Change

Throughout the discussion of ethnic relations in social studies classes, it should be stressed continually that in a nation like the United States, which is legally committed to such social values as equality of opportunity, achievement in employment, and universal political participation, the conditions confronting those who occupy the lower strata of the occupational, political, and economic hierarchies are susceptible to the development of a high degree of social alienation. As a result of its commitment to such goals, a nation leads all of its citizens to expect social equality; but since society generates and sustains economic and political conditions of inequality, it produces resentment and hostility among those groups that do not achieve their expectations.[14]

Throughout the present century, certain basic reasons for this social inequality in the United States have been quite evident. Of these, the most fundamental is the racial attitude and collective behavior of white Americans toward black Americans and other ethnic minority groups. Racial prejudice and discrimination has shaped our nation's development decisively; it continues to threaten our future. The behavioral characteristics of white racism are essentially responsible for the recent volatile racial and ethnic disorders which have erupted, many times violently, in the nation's urban areas. Among the reasons for these social problems are:

1. Pervasive discrimination and segregation in employment, education, and housing, which has resulted in the continuing exclusion of great numbers of minority-group members from the benefits of economic progress and social mobility.
2. Minority-group in-migration and white exodus, which in combination have produced the massive and increasing densities of impoverished minorities in the central cities of our metropolitan areas, creating an increasing crisis of deteriorating educational, recreational, health, and service facilities.
3. The nonwhite ethnic ghettos, primarily black on a nationwide basis, where segregation and economic poverty converge on the young to destroy opportunity, encourage failure, and reinforce racial hatred. Crime, drug addiction, dependency on welfare, and bitterness and resentment against society in general, and white society in particular, are the result.

Paralleling these extremely negative situations is the fact that most whites, and some minority peoples outside the inner cities, have enjoyed a level of economic, social, and political prosperity previously unknown in the history of civilization. For more than a generation this affluence has been flaunted through television and other media before the disadvantaged minority youth, resulting in an era of continual racial inferiority and bitterness.

Minority-Group Behavior

A primary objective of the social studies program is to familiarize students with the manner in which minority-group alienation develops into open conflict and is ramified throughout society. As is being portrayed continually, when minority-group conflict results in legal disorder, such disorder commonly receives national publicity and may initiate an atmosphere of widespread "lawlessness" that extends far beyond the significance of a particular incident. Indeed, such isolated instances of violence and conflict have generated the attitude of a general social crisis among large segments of the public and, thereby, have reinforced the negative racist view on the part of substantial portions of the white population to a much greater extent than if the alienated had had available the proper means of legal or political expression.

Consequently, the awareness of violence and overt conflict further intensifies the emotions of racial hatred and prejudice that, historically, have been largely responsible for the disadvantaged position of minority groups in the United States.[15] Thus, this so-called white backlash promotes a dichotomy of attitudes that magnifies particular isolated conflicts as far as racial warfare on a global scale.

There appears little doubt that one of the foremost tasks confronting the American educational system is to instill within youth the attitude that it is absolutely vital to meet the legitimate demands and aspirations of all ethnic groups and, thus, direct the vast collective capabilities of all segments of American society into positive channels in the national interest. Furthermore, it is vital that urban and suburban social studies programs be broadened by introducing the quality of social relevancy, which, most unfortunately, has been overshadowed by the contemporary emphasis placed upon academic achievement—achievement which has little to do with solving the crucial social problems presently confronting this nation. Social studies teachers must comprehend that instilling proper attitudes and promoting an awareness among students of cultural diversity and differences are assets in a democratic society. Encouraging such attitudes is just as significant an instructional objective as the teaching of traditional academic skills and, quite possibly, will have a more positive future effect on student development as well as upon societal maturation.

Assumptions for Student Inquiry

1. In the United States, during the past and continuing at present, the integration of racial minority groups has been primarily locational rather than psychological in nature. Furthermore, there is every indication that this situation will continue throughout the foreseeable future.

2. Where policies of cultural integration or assimilation are enforced, minority groups will have to sacrifice their cultural traditions and value systems and accept the cultural values of the majority group.

3. The ultimate reason for integration of the races in any nation is national security, since no nation can afford significant minority segments which possess values and traditions divergent from those held by the majority.

4. To emphasize integration among the races in a locational or economic sense will only fall far short of achieving the ultimate goal of socializing or assimilating the various demographic elements comprising American society.

5. Minority-group peoples must be accepted in a psychological sense by the vast majority of the white population before the terms *civil rights* and *integration* will have any valid meaning in the United States.

6. The major factor preventing the successful assimilation of the Negro, Mexican-American, American Indian, Puerto Rican, and Oriental into American society, unlike members of ethnic groups from Western Europe, is the visibility of skin color.

7. Racial and cultural assimilation can only be successfully achieved on a total basis through intermarriage of all diverse ethnic groups, including the white race.

8. Policies of integration which result in a greater degree of tolerance of the majority for the minority-group peoples are certainly not the ultimate goal of integration in the United States.

9. The only way in which minority peoples can develop their own cultural traditions and achieve their highest potentials is to be segregated from the majority group.

10. The only valid policy for promoting equal opportunity for minority-group peoples in various nations, including the United States, is to promote a policy of apartheid, similar to that in South Africa, where each minority group is given its own geographic area and economic base.

THE CHANGING ROLE OF WOMEN

During the fall of 1974, the Los Angeles public school district introduced a new textbook series in the elementary social studies curriculum entitled *Free to Be: You and Me.* [16] This series, developed for primary and intermediate age youth and published by McGraw-Hill, is designed to acquaint children with various careers which might fascinate them regardless of the vocational roles imposed by sex stereotyping in the traditional educational environment. The textbook series is expected to be adopted by other school districts as educators move away from sex stereotyping materials in the era of women's liberation—an era which represents a movement away from sexism and toward personhood (in this particular instance, a representation of the free children's movement).

The Women's Liberation Movement

In today's society, the traditional characteristics which determine what constitutes manhood and womanhood are being challenged by both women and men. Every effort is being made to portray how the female and male roles in society have been stereotyped through the formal educational system, literature, music, the movies, television, and so on. Regardless of individual opinions concerning these efforts, students should be provided the opportunity to examine the institutions that have perpetuated the artificial masculine and feminine behavior patterns in American society.

The women's liberation movement, as exemplified by such national organizations as the Ms. Foundation for Women, would appear to be one of the foremost instruments for social change that this nation has ever witnessed. As such, it deserves to be a major theme for analysis in the contemporary social studies curriculum.

A major theme for student awareness is that within a democratic society, social change is the foundation of democracy and, thus, is a constant evolutionary process. Nevertheless, all social reform movements which attain national status, such as women's liberation, generate a considerable degree of controversy both within the movement itself and outside the movement among diverse segments of society. Moreover, such controversy is imminent when the particular movement involves relatively large numbers of people, when it is influential in determining policies of the national, state, and local governments, and when it possesses the potential for altering significantly a traditional value system of society.

The Rationale for Women's Liberation

Even though students will continue to hear statements representing radical, moderate, and opposing views concerning the necessity for such social reform, they should achieve an understanding of several of the basic themes which provide the major arguments expounded by the proponents of women's liberation. An effective instructional technique would be to provide for in-depth student examination of several of the primary issues involved. The immediate responsibilities of the social studies instructor, as is the case when considering any controversial issue, are those of motivating student interest and facilitating as objective a classroom discussion as possible.

The current women's liberation movement, which gained nationwide recognition in the late 1960s, is a complex and all-encompassing social movement which is attempting to move women toward economic, legal, political, psychological, social, and, it would seem, even biological equality with men. Commonly referred to by a number of terms, including the "feminist movement," "female liberation," and the "women's rights movement," the present scope of this movement has been described as "the aggregate force exerted by an unknown number of groups of two or more women who firmly believe that they are discriminated against solely because they are female."[17]

It is vital for students to understand that the present-day movement for women to seek a nontraditional life-style has significant historical precedent. More than a half-century ago, American women achieved a degree of equality when they won the right to vote under the Nineteenth Amendment. This historic suffrage legislation, passed in 1920, had its inception at a Women's Right's Convention in Seneca Falls, New York, shortly before the middle of the nineteenth century (1848).[18]

During the decade of the 1960s, three major events occurred to provide substantial encouragement and thrust to the movement, which for more than a century included but a handful of active supporters. First, a highly influential book entitled *The Feminine Mystique,* published in 1963, provided an ideological foundation for disenchanted women. The author, Betty Friedan, provided a militant call to American women to overcome the shackles imposed on them by a male-dominated society. A recurrent theme of this publication, and of the many publications which were to follow dealing with this topic, was that being a "career" homemaker—that is, a wife and mother—stifles the female's psychological growth, particularly the quest for self-fulfillment.

Also during 1963, President John F. Kennedy established the Commission on the Status of Women. This commission further illuminated the many problems confronting women, particularly in the economic sectors of society. Significantly, many of the recommendations stated by this commission resulted in the inclusion of prohibitions against sex discrimination in Title VII of the Civil Rights Act. This title requires that all employers treat all present and potential employees on an equal basis without regard to sex in every phase of employment.[19] A procedure for promoting awareness of the national impact of this legislation would be for students to examine the numerous advertisements seeking employees, submitted by potential employers representing every economic sector, in newspapers, employment registers, and placement bulletins since 1970 which include the employment classification, "An Equal Opportunity-Affirmative Action Employer."

The third recent event which gave great impetus to the cause of women's liberation was the civil rights movement of the mid-1960s. If blacks and other ethnic minorities were able to achieve more economic, political, and social status by publicly pronouncing their views regarding discrimination, there was justifiable reason for women to utilize the same strategy.

Women's Liberation in Future Perspective

Regardless of the pronouncements of several of the radical feminist organizations throughout the nation, the essence of the women's liberation movement involved two major issues by the mid-1970s. The first is in the economic sphere and revolves around equal employment opportunities. There is overwhelming evidence, on the basis of countless surveys, that women have not succeeded as well in the job market as their male counterparts. This apparent discrimination is particularly evident in those careers and professions which are highly rewarding in terms of responsibility, income, and prestige. Specifically, the male-female imbalances in such fields as management, medicine, law, and university teaching are many times cited as examples of the economic imbalance. Closely related to the problem of discrimination regarding the opportunity to pursue certain careers, is a major issue of complaint that women receive unequal pay in comparison to men for identical work.

Significantly, American higher education, with substantial justification, has been, and continues to be, widely criticized for its traditional practices on both counts. Obviously, women cannot enter certain careers or professions unless they receive formal training. The professional schools of medicine, law, and business have, historically, been extremely reluctant to admit women to their programs. As a result of recent legislative pressures, however, this situation is presently changing and should continue to change during the future. Second, there is pronounced feminist discontent concerning both the employment practices and the reward system of higher education itself. While women have always comprised a proportion of the instructional faculties of colleges and universities (on a comparable basis with medicine and law, the college-teaching profession has not been as "closed" to women), they have always represented a minority. A more central issue, however, is that institutions of higher education have definitely discriminated against women through their promotional policies, which have given preferential treatment to males over females when granting academic rank, tenure, and salary. Similarly, both of these discriminatory practices are rapidly diminishing. The second major issue of the women's liberation movement, which had received widespread support by the mid-1970s, involves the legal rights of women. The advocates of the thesis that the law provides unequal treatment for women based their case upon discriminatory legal practices in family law, property law, criminal law, abortion, and government benefits.[20] However, since the problem of legal inequity involves such complex issues as alimony and child-support statutes under existing legislation, it will not be as readily resolved during the near future as the inequities in education and employment practices.

At this point in the discussion, students should be provided the opportunity to examine in detail the recent legislation that will have a decided social impact now and in the future. Specifically, students should be encouraged to analyze the Equal Rights Amendment, which most assuredly will become the Twenty-seventh Amendment to the United States Constitution, the Equal Opportunity Act, and the various laws which prohibit sexual bias in any educational program receiving federal financial assistance. As a concluding class activity, students might evaluate the many accomplishments achieved by the women's liberation movement during the last decade in comparison with the relative lack of progress made during the preceding century, and might attempt to offer several valid explanations for the movement's current successes.

Assumptions for Student Inquiry

1. Like America's minority ethnic groups, the female population has been seriously discriminated against with regard to economic opportunities and many of the basic human freedoms during the first two centuries of development in the United States.
2. Throughout the history of the United States, the female proportion of the population

has been faced with much less discrimination in all areas of human activity than women in any other of the world's nations.

3. The women's liberation movement represents one of the most significant movements for social reform that has been witnessed in the United States during the nation's two-hundred-year history.

4. The contemporary women's liberation movement will prove to be just another in a series of short-lived attempts at social reform which will result in little, if any, reduction of discrimination against the American female.

5. Since the American female population is not being discriminated against, the women's liberation movement, in actuality, represents a small minority of radical and militant females who have created an artificial or false cause for their own personal reasons and benefit.

6. The current wave of feminism will contribute significantly to a decline of the birth rate throughout the remainder of the present century as many women continue to challenge their traditional social roles as mother and homemaker.

CRIME AND VIOLENCE

There is no human behavioral pattern as negative in total impact as the problem of crime and violence confronting urban America. Crime is a social problem with many facets and does not lend itself to an easy solution.

Crime as a Behavioral Characteristic

One major theme which should run throughout a discussion of this topic in social studies classes is that incidents of crime and violence are not just sordid happenings—they reflect both social and individual behavior patterns. As one national authority on the subject recently stated, "Crime reflects the character of a people."[21] This will continue to be a difficult fact for our society to comprehend, since there is no simple remedy for defective character.

Students should understand that the capacity to commit crime is a consequence resulting from all the qualities in life that determine what individuals are. Heredity and the physical and cultural environment, the interaction between the individual and society, the totality of human nature and human experience, all contribute to the potential for committing crime. Thus, crime reflects more than the emotional ill health of the extremely small proportion of the population who commit it. To a significant extent it reflects the character of our contemporary society.[22]

Students should be encouraged to give thoughtful attention to the premise that criminals are largely the products of their social environment. Thus, crime is directly linked to all of the ills plaguing our society. Crime and violence are symptomatic of a wide range of underlying social problems. Students will attain little understanding of crime unless they are familiar with the environment in which it breeds, especially the physical and social environment of the central cities of the nation's large urban areas. Instead of reading and discussing these problems in the abstract, every opportunity must be provided for students to observe the dehumanizing influence on the individual of poverty, of unemployment, of slums, of malnutrition, of sickness and disease, of alcoholism and narcotics addiction, of child neglect, of prostitution, of pollution, of anxiety, hatred, hopelessness, and injustice. These elements provide the foundation for crime and violence in the inner-city environment and economically depressed rural areas.

It is vital, however, for students to be aware of some of the difficulties which arise when attempting to explain the reasons for crime and violence in such absolute terms. Although most behavioral scientists agree that crime is concentrated among the lower socioeconomic classes, they appear somewhat hesitant to accept the premise that the lack of affluence and of political-social influence is a major reason for this concentration. Indeed, there exists the popular assumption that poverty is not the most significant characteristic of the lower class with respect to crime. Since the impoverished classes lack other things in addition to money, such as education, mental and physical health, ambition, and stable family life, behavioral scientists have been free to select various dimensions in explaining the high crime rate among these individuals.[23]

The Broad Concept of Crime

Those who define criminal acts as uneducated, unskilled, "lower-class" behavior have considerable difficulty explaining the crimes committed by middle- and upper-class individuals and groups. The widespread existence of this situation provides students with a second highly relevant theme for analysis. For instance, students should examine the following types of crime and attempt to suggest possible causes:

1. White-collar crime, which results in losses of billions of dollars annually in tax evasion, price fixing, consumer fraud, embezzlement, and so on.
2. Organized crime, which collects hundreds of millions from gambling, loansharking, illegal drug traffic, extortion, prostitution, political corruption, and other criminal activities.
3. Crimes of passion, which include most homicides, rapes, and assaults.
4. Violations of laws designed to protect public health and safety, such as traffic regulations, construction codes, fire ordinances, minimum standards of safety and quality.
5. Revolutionary crime intended to promote rioting and mob violence and terrorist actions such as bombing and sniping.
6. Corruption in government at all levels, including conflicts of interest, bribes, payoffs, and fixes.
7. Police crime, such as brutality, wrongful arrest, and blackmail.

Obviously, the types and methods of crime and violence are as varied as human behavior in our complex and rapidly changing society. During this turbulent era in our national development, when youth seriously questions the purpose, the integrity, and the effectiveness of our laws, teachers must continually emphasize that nothing is worthwhile for the individual or for his society unless his or her own actions are honest in all forms of behavior.

Assumptions for Student Inquiry

1. As the United States continues to experience urban growth, the rate of all types of criminal activity will also continue to increase.
2. The only way to substantially reduce many types of violent crime in the United States is through legislation which will make it unlawful for citizens to purchase any type of firearm or other potentially lethal weapon.
3. Organized criminal activities, such as illicit drug traffic, extortion, political corruption, and prostitution, could be halted immediately if many of the nation's public officials themselves were not involved directly or indirectly in such illegal activities.
4. Unlike democratic societies, such as the United States, only totalitarian governments or police states are capable of preventing both individual and organized crime.
5. As long as the United States remains a free and democratic society, the nation will continue to experience all types of criminal activities.
6. If zero population growth is achieved in the early twenty-first century and the average age of the population increases, the rate of juvenile delinquency and other types of crime will decrease since today approximately one-third of all crimes are attributed to people under eighteen years of age, and there will be proportionately fewer young people.

ORGANIZED RELIGION

In a democratic society, the responsibility of the social studies is to acquaint students with various global religions and the impact that religion has had upon the social and national development of the United States, as well as upon the development of other cultures, rather than to emphasize religious instruction per se. With regard to the problem of teaching about religion in the American public education system, a recent United States Supreme Court opinion stated that "one's education is not complete without a study of comparative religion or the history of religion and its relationship to the advancement of civilization."[24] Since religion has been and continues to be a basic phenomenon influencing the economic, political, and social development of individuals and societies, it will continue to be an important component of the social studies curriculum. However, before students can comprehend the contemporary impact of religion on other cultures, it would seem that emphasis should be placed upon a consideration of the role of religion in American society.

The Functional Analysis of Religion in America

Rather than asking students to inquire into the origins or the truth of the principal religious faiths in America—Protestantism, Catholicism, and Judaism—the instructor should encourage students to consider what functions the institution of organized religion fulfills for both individuals and society as a whole, and how institutions of religion are related to other institutions of society. Behavioral scientists commonly distinguish several specific aspects of religion's function of providing meaning and reinforcing motivation in the face of human fear, uncertainty, hopelessness, and tragedy when these elements might otherwise alienate men from society.[25]

Religion, however, involves obligation. Such obligation may sanctify the norms and values of society. However, to the extent that it does, the element of obligation contributes to social stability and control. On the other hand, religion may encourage ethical demands which result in criticism of the values and practices of society. In addition, religion performs important identity functions for individuals. For example, religious identification as Protestants, Catholics, or Jews has become a means of developing group identification as well as group participation in total society. Thus, civil religion has become a mode of participation in the "American way of life."[26]

Perhaps the primary theme for student analysis involves the premise that the purpose of organized religion in the United States is to reconcile the individual to his fate. According to this precept, the ultimate function of religion is to provide a meaning for life. Death confronts every human and religion attempts to reconcile him to his destiny. Human beings need some assurance in order to survive the human condition, as they experience suffering and death and know that they themselves will eventually confront the same fate. Man lives under conditions of uncertainty, when his health, safety, economic security, and his life may be lost at a moment's notice. Furthermore, in many instances man is powerless to control his destiny. For most people there exists no apparent way out of these circumstances. The characteristics of uncertainty and powerlessness result in the necessity for an institution that emphasizes the "transcendental" experience—something beyond the realm of everyday life.

The religious institutions resulting from this central concept assume a variety of forms. Within the United States the structure of religion has varied from the elaborate rituals of the Catholic Church to the simple ceremonies of many Protestant denominations. Regardless of the procedural and structural differences, the basic religious function is to provide the individual with spiritual solace in relation to supernatural forces.

The Status of Traditional Religion

A meaningful technique for motivating student interest in the institution of religion is to encourage a discussion involving some of the reasons as to why the principal religious faiths in America—Protestantism, Catholicism, and Judaism —each are currently evidencing signs of weakness and membership decline, particularly with regard to new memberships among young people under thirty years of age. When compared to the total population, no single church even remotely approaches having on its membership rolls a majority of the nation's people. During the past two decades each of the major religious denominations has continued to decline substantially, with Roman Catholicism experiencing a membership decrease of approximately 40 percent among young people.

Of all religious groups in the United States, the largest increases in membership among youth in recent years have been noted among the Holiness and Pentecostal sects, which are outside the mainstream of American Protestantism, as well as certain Asian religions, of which Zen Buddhism appears to be the most significant. There exists the assumption that the newer religions, and particularly the Asian religious sects, have gained increasing popularity among the young probably due in part to their nonpolitical orientation and their emphasis upon human relationships in the context of life on earth, rather than on salvation and everlasting life after death.[27] Furthermore, while not accepting different religious affiliations, many have become discontented with the apparent apathy of the traditional Christian religions toward domestic racial problems, war, poverty, and other social and economic issues confronting the nation. Further calamitous social and economic conditions could result in the emergence of nontraditional religious groups of substantial size, which could, under certain circumstances, result in sufficient social agitation to significantly change the traditional model of American religion. For instance, the emergence of the Black Muslims exemplifies the type of religious extremism that could evolve on a much larger scale.

The probability is that traditional organized religion in the United States will not increase substantially in the foreseeable future. To the contrary, the churches will probably continue to lose their appeal to the young and, therefore, national influence, but they probably will not dwindle in membership to the extent of becoming largely ineffectual. The emergence of such youth groups as the "Jesus People" will contain enough elements of tradition to maintain Christianity throughout this contemporary evolutionary period in American development, even though, perhaps, in a different social context.

To conclude a discussion of the role of religion in contemporary American society, students could be asked to present their views regarding the following questions:

1. What are some of the reasons that religion is so vitally important in the lives of so many Americans?
2. What are some of the reasons that traditional organized religion has apparently lost much of its appeal for many young people in the United States today?
3. What are some of the fundamental differences between the traditional Christian religion and the major Asian religions, such as Buddhism, Confucianism, and Taoism?
4. Why do non-Christian religions, such as several of the Asian religions, appear to possess a great deal of appeal for an increasing number of younger people in the United States?
5. Why does traditional religion appear to have more of an impact upon the personal lives and behavior of individuals residing in rural areas and smaller communities in the United States than it seems to have in large urban areas?

Assumptions for Student Inquiry

1. As a greater proportion of the population of a nation attains a higher level of

education, the organized religious institutions of that nation reflect a decrease in memberships and followers.

2. One of the basic reasons that Christianity has lost much of its appeal for younger people in the United States is the fact that its basic religious teachings or tenets must be accepted on faith rather than upon evidence or proof.

3. A second major reason that organized Christianity has suffered, and continues to suffer, decreasing popularity in the United States is that its basic principles emphasize salvation after death rather than placing a priority upon life upon earth.

4. One of the primary reasons why certain Asian religions have gained popularity in the United States is that these religions emphasize the improvement of human relationships on earth rather than everlasting life after death.

5. Names or titles applied to particular religions are of little significance, since any set of ideas, theory, philosophy, or faith that helps a person attain order, direction, and justification for his or her existence is all that is necessary.

POLITICAL SOCIALIZATION IN A DEMOCRACY

The claim that the ultimate goal of American public education is the development of good citizens for a democratic society continues to be one of the most frequently stated objectives in the literature of professional education. Furthermore, of all of the subject areas comprising the secondary curriculum, the social studies program is the most directly responsible for the transmission of the values and attitudes that should characterize a good "democratic citizen." Thus, the central function of the social studies program is synonymous with the ultimate objectives of American education insofar as it is the curricular area responsible for the development and perpetuation of those elements of the nation's cultural heritage which will result in promoting strong feelings of loyalty and patriotism among the nation's inhabitants and, hence, a high degree of national viability and cohesion.

An effective strategy for motivating interest and promoting a discussion of patriotism or nationalism would be for the instructor to ask students to determine what personal behavioral characteristics should be possessed by a "good" citizen in today's continually evolving society. Second, have students present their views regarding what type of individual would characterize a "good" citizen of the Soviet Union or the People's Republic of China. Third, ask students to enumerate some of the behavioral differences which exist between "good" citizens in democratic societies and in totalitarian societies. Fourth, ask students what they consider to be the major or ultimate objectives of the social studies program in every nation which has an established formal, compulsory, mass coeducational system of public education.

The Development of Democratic Citizenship

An extremely popular view of the primary role of social studies education in the United States is that this curricular area should prepare students to achieve competency for actual participation in democratic processes. According to this premise, a basic objective—if not the foremost objective—of social education should be that of inculcating youth with a comprehension and appreciation of the political character of their society, its procedural operation, and the national goals and aspirations.[28] Obviously, every modern society requires a trained or highly skilled populace if the nation is to maintain both its national viability and its international prestige.

In a democratic society like the United States, however, it is vital to the nation's continued domestic and international development that its citizenry be educated, as opposed to trained, and possess a highly knowledgeable understanding of the complexities of the democratic process. In many instances, the populace of a democracy has a direct influence upon policy decisions involving national and international affairs. Thus, both the democratic structure and the level of our national development will erode unless youth are knowledgeable of democratic institutions and motivated to fulfill their political responsibilities as adults.

Dissent and Political Socialization in a Democracy

A major responsibility of the social studies instructor should be one of promoting an understanding of the function of political dissent in a democratic society. The emphasis should be placed upon encouraging students to determine some of the inherent differences between responsible and irresponsible dissent. A basic principle to stress throughout the social studies curriculum is that in a nation like ours, social, political, and economic change is oftentimes the result of political dissent by a significant proportion of society within the broad limits of the democratic process.

Furthermore, students should understand that the right of conscientious dissent against political authority is a fundamental freedom guaranteed by our democratic system. Indeed, this human right is one of the most basic characteristics that distinguishes a democracy from a totalitarian state. To a large degree, this rationale for political dissent challenges the traditional philosophy that social education must serve as the curricular agent for the transmission of the nation's cultural heritage for the purpose of emphasizing only the positive elements of the nation's historical, political, and social development.[29] Given the many crucial issues that will continue to confront our nation during future decades, it would seem imperative that social studies teachers encourage students to become aware of the inconsistencies, inequalities, and inequities which have characterized the nation's development, and which continue to exist within American society, and, thereby, prepare them to take part in resolving these problems through active participation in the various social "movements" which are based upon dissent against the more negative social attitudes and instructions which prevail within our nation today.

Assumptions for Student Inquiry

1. The ultimate objective or purpose of the secondary social studies curriculum in this nation is synonymous with the ultimate objective of the American educational system: that of developing citizens for a democratic society.

2. The social studies program is the only curricular area in the educational system which has the direct responsibility for the development of good citizens for a democratic society.

3. The purpose of the social studies or social education curriculum is the same in the United States, the Soviet Union, the People's Republic of China, and every other nation that possesses a formal education system: that of developing good citizens who will strive to achieve the national goals and objectives of each particular nation.

4. A good citizen in a democratic society is one who accepts the traditionally established social, political, and economic attitudes held by the majority of the people and accepts what his governmental agencies tell him and reacts accordingly.

5. A good citizen in a democratic society is one who rejects and dissents against the traditional social, political, and economic attitudes and values held by a majority of the people and constantly engages in active dissent against the policies of government and other administrative agencies.

6. A good citizen in a democratic society is an individual who continually studies and examines the traditional social, economic, and political values and ideals held by the majority of society and who, after careful consideration of this value in relation to the rapidly changing needs of society, engages in conscientious dissent, sometimes active and sometimes passive but always within the broad limits of the democratic process, depending upon the nature of the particular issue or governmental policy.

7. Since the democratic form of government is such a unique and complex process, it is impossible to specifically define what type of citizen possesses the characteristics of a good citizen in a democratic society.

8. The greatest strength that a democratic form of government possesses, and the characteristic that will insure its continued existence in contrast to totalitarian and dictatorial forms of government, is the right the citizenry has to continually dissent against the policies and programs of the various governmental agencies at the federal, state, and local levels.

9. Since the United States is continually attempting to develop and refine its democratic system, the nation cannot as yet afford dissent from too large a segment of society in the interests of national security, viability, and unity. During the foreseeable future, therefore, dissent must be limited to a small minority.

10. In a democratic society, all dissent, whether expounded by individuals or groups, must be expressed within the limits of the existing laws.

SUMMARY

Throughout the remainder of the twentieth century, every effort must be made to place a priority upon the development of a humanistic curriculum, particularly in social studies education. As our urban-technological society becomes more complex, the social studies program must assume the primary responsibility for developing within youth the two basic behavioral characteristics of self-realization and emotional maturity. A major objective in curriculum planning, therefore, must be to increase the emphasis placed upon the study of the behavioral sciences in secondary education, so that today's students can learn to live and work successfully in a constantly changing social environment.

Notes

CHAPTER 1

1. Edwin Fenton, *Teaching the New Social Studies in Secondary Schools* (New York: Holt, Rinehart & Winston, 1966), p. 366.
2. E. Grey Dimond, "Educating the Future Physician," *Saturday Review/World,* October 1973, p. 52.
3. Bernard Berelson, ed., *The Behavioral Sciences Today* (New York: Basic Books, 1963), p. 4.
4. Ibid., p. 2.
5. National Academy of Sciences, *The Behavioral and Social Sciences: Outlook and Needs* (Englewood Cliffs, N.J.: Prentice-Hall, 1970), p. 69.
6. Meyer F. Nimkoff, "Anthropology, Sociology, and Social Psychology," in Erling M. Hunt et al., *High School Social Studies Perspectives,* cited in Fenton, *Teaching the New Social Studies,* p. 368.
7. Ibid., pp. 368–73.
8. Excellent practical definitions of the behavioral sciences for secondary school students are contained in *The Behavioral and Social Sciences,* pp. 27–49 passim.
9. Ibid., p. 28.
10. Ibid., pp. 28–29.
11. One of the most concise examinations of the role of social psychology as a behavioral science is presented in Edwin P. Hollander, *Principles and Methods of Social Psychology* (New York: Oxford University Press, 1967), pp. 4–7.
12. Ibid., pp. 6–7.
13. A brief but excellent discussion of the development of sociology as a field of study in the United States is presented in Peter L. Berger and Brigitte Berger, *Sociology: A Biographical Approach* (New York: Basic Books, 1972), p. 36.
14. Ibid., pp. 357–60.

CHAPTER 2

1. For a thorough account of the role of the social studies curriculum in the contemporary American educational system, see Randall C. Anderson, *Current Trends in Secondary School Social Studies* (Lincoln, Nebr.: Professional Educators Publications, 1972), pp. 14–18.
2. Morris R. Lewenstein, *Teaching Social Studies in Junior and Senior High Schools* (Chicago: Rand McNally, 1963), pp. 50–51.
3. Jonathan C. McLendon, *Social Studies in Secondary Education* (New York: Macmillan, 1965), pp. 67–68.
4. Donald W. Oliver, "The Selection of Content in the Social Sciences," in Edwin Fenton, *Teaching the New Social Studies in Secondary Schools* (New York: Holt, Rinehart & Winston, 1966), p. 99.

5. Ibid.

6. Bernard Berelson and Gary A. Steiner, "Methods of Inquiry," cited in Fenton, *Teaching the New Social Studies,* p. 190.

7. Ibid.

8. Ibid., p. 193.

9. Ibid., pp. 194–95.

10. Gary Manson et al., "Social Studies Curriculum Guidelines," *Social Education* 35, no. 8 (December 1971): 853–69.

11. Ibid., pp. 855–60.

12. Ibid., p. 856.

13. Ibid.

14. Ibid.

15. Ibid., p. 857.

16. Ibid.

17. Ibid., pp. 858–59.

18. Ibid., pp. 859–60.

19. Anderson, *Secondary School Social Studies,* p. 14.

CHAPTER 3

1. L. Thomas Hopkins, "The Overlooked Factor," *Phi Delta Kappan* 55, no. 10 (June 1974): 694.

2. Ibid.

3. For an excellent examination of the vital topic of thought in social education, see Hilda Taba, "Implementing Thinking as an Objective in Social Studies," cited in *Effective Thinking in the Social Studies,* ed. Jean Fair and Fannie R. Shaftel, 37th Yearbook, National Council for the Social Studies (Washington, 1967), pp. 25–26, and Randall C. Anderson, "Introducing the World Population Crises to Secondary Social Studies Classes: An Inquiry-Oriented Instructional Strategy," *Social Education* 34, no. 1 (January 1970): 27–28.

4. Two highly significant views on values clarification in contemporary social studies education are contained in Gary Manson et al., "Social Studies Curriculum Guidelines," *Social Education* 35, no. 8 (December 1971): 858–59, and Jerrold R. Coombs, "Objectives of Value Analysis," cited in *Values Education: Rationale, Strategies and Procedures,* ed. Lawrence E. Metcalf, 41st Yearbook, National Council for the Social Studies (Washington, 1971), pp. 1–3.

5. An excellent statement on the decision-making process is found in *Society and Mankind* (White Plains, N.Y.: Center for Humanities, 1974), p. 4. See also Jerrold R. Coombs and Milton Meux, "Teaching Strategies for Value Analysis," cited in Metcalf, *Values Education,* pp. 29–37 passim.

6. *Society and Mankind,* p. 6.

7. Ibid., p. 4.

8. Ibid., p. 2.

9. Perhaps the best recent statement concerning the instructional objective of social participation is contained in Manson et al., "Social Studies Curriculum Guidelines," pp. 859–60.

10. Ibid., p. 856–57.

11. W. David Maxwell, "PBTE: A Case of the Emperor's New Clothes," *Phi Delta Kappan* 55, no. 5 (January 1974): 307.

12. Allen A. Schmieder, *Competency-Based Teacher Education* (Washington: American Association of Colleges for Teacher Education and ERIC Clearinghouse of Teacher Education, 1973), cited in Benjamin Rosner and Patricia M. Kay, "Will the Promise of C/PBTE Be Fulfilled?" *Phi Delta Kappan,* 55, no. 5 (January 1974): 290.

13. Ibid.

14. For example, see *Competencies for Social Studies Teachers* (Topeka: Kansas State Department of Education, Division of Instruction, 1974). Also, the entire January 1974 issue of *Phi Delta Kappan* is devoted to pertinent discussions of competency/performance-based teacher education.

CHAPTER 4

1. Edward S. Cornish, "Responses of Leaders in the Study of the Future," *Social Education* 36, no. 3 (March 1972): 245.

2. *Society and Mankind* (White Plains, N.Y.: Center for Humanities, 1974), p. 8.

3. Cornish, "Responses of Leaders," pp. 244–45.

4. An excellent description of activities to promote student interest in futuristic studies is contained in a statement entitled "What Can Social Studies Teachers Do to Help Prepare Their Students for the Future?" *Social Education,* 36, no. 3 (March 1972): 243–46.

5. Thomas Malthus, *An Essay on the Principle of Population as It Affects the Future Improvement of Mankind,* 1798. The basic thesis of this publication was that population increases faster than the means of subsistence and, therefore, must be controlled either by checking the rate of human reproduction or by maintaining high death rates.

6. "World Population Projections: 1965–2000," *Population Bulletin,* October 1965, p. 90.

7. *Population Bulletin,* December 1970, p. 11.

8. Ibid., June 1970, p. 3.

9. Wayne Davis, "Overpopulated America," cited in *Population: A Clash of Prophets,* ed. Edward Pohlman (New York: New American Library, 1973), p. 94.

10. Commission on Population Growth and the American Future, "Resources and the Environment," cited in Pohlman, *Population,* p. 223.

11. Zero population growth (or z.p.g.) for the United States equals a two-child family, since under current conditions of infant mortality, an average of about 2.1 children per female would, in several decades, result in stable population increase.

12. Julian Simon, "Science Does Not Show That There Is Overpopulation in the U.S. —or Elsewhere," cited in Pohlman, *Population,* pp. 58–61.

13. *Christian Science Monitor,* May 26, 1973, *Kansas City Star,* March 24, 1974.

14. *Kansas City Star,* May 17, 1973.

15. Ibid., March 24, 1974.

16. Numerous current global population statistics are presented in each monthly issue of the *Population Bulletin.*

17. Ibid.

18. Paul Ehrlich, "The Population Crises: 1970's Style," cited in Pohlman, *Population,* p. 17.

19. Randall C. Anderson, *Current Trends in Secondary School Social Studies* (Lincoln, Nebr.: Professional Educators Publications, 1972), pp. 61–62.

20. A. J. Meyer, "Energy: Need We Worry? Yes . . . ," *Christian Science Monitor,* October 10, 1972.

21. Ibid.

22. Ibid.

23. Ibid.

24. John D. Chapman, "Interaction between Man and His Resources," cited in National Academy of Sciences, *Resources and Man* (San Francisco: W. H. Freeman, 1969), p. 32.

25. Avery M. Guest, "Whose Environmental Crises?" cited in Pohlman, *Population,* p. 177.

26. Ibid., p. 229.

27. Ibid., pp. 229–30.

28. "The Green Revolution, Peace and Humanity," *Population Bulletin,* Selection no. 35 (1970), p. 1.

29. Harold G. Shane, "The Coming Global Famine," *Phi Delta Kappan* 56 no. 1 (September 1974): 36.

30. A brief but contemporary interpretation of Malthusian doctrine is presented in Rhoads Murphy, *The Scope of Geography* (Chicago: Rand McNally, 1969), pp. 158–59.

31. Ibid.

32. Randall C. Anderson, "Introducing the World Population Crises to Secondary Social Studies Classes: An Inquiry-Oriented Instructional Strategy," *Social Education* 34, no. 1 (January 1970): 32.

33. Ibid., p. 33.

34. Ibid.

35. *United Nations Demographic Yearbook* (New York, 1968), table 7.

36. The United Nations Economic and Social Council designated 1974 World Population Year.

CHAPTER 5

1. Saul D. Feldman and Gerald W. Thielbar, eds., *Life Styles: Diversity in American Society* (Boston: Little, Brown, 1972), p. 1.

2. Ibid., p. 2.

3. A brief but excellent discussion of this topic is presented in Louis J. Karmel, "Sex Education No! Sex Education Yes!" *Phi Delta Kappan* 52, no. 2 (October 1970): 95–96.

4. Alfred C. Kinsey and Paul H. Gebhard, *Sexual Behavior in the Human Female* (Philadelphia: W. B. Saunders, 1953).

5. A most informative current source for social studies instructors, which examines the assumption that American society is presently witnessing a sexual revolution, is John N. Edwards, *Sex and Society* (Chicago: 1972).

6. Ibid., p. 17.

7. Ibid.

8. Isadore Rubin, "Transition in Sex Values—Implications for the Education of Adolescents," cited in *Sexual Development and Behavior: Selected Readings,* ed. Anne Juhasz (Homewood, Ill.: Dorsey Press, 1973), p. 213.

9. Ibid., p. 211.

10. *Washington Star News,* cited in *Wichita Eagle and Beacon,* June 5, 1974.

11. Maurice Leznoff and William A. Westley, "The Homosexual Community," cited in Edwards, *Sex and Society,* p. 79.

12. "Playboy Panel: Homosexuality," *Playboy* 18, no. 4 (April 1971): 63.

13. Ibid.

14. New York Times News Service, cited in *Wichita Eagle and Beacon,* April 6, 1974.

15. Ibid., June 12, 1974.

16. *Playboy* 21, no. 6 (June 1974): 61.

17. A national committee appointed by President Richard Nixon for the purpose of analyzing the effects of "pornographic" and "obscene" materials upon behavior patterns.

18. For instance, see the recent Supreme Court decision which places the responsibility of defining "pornographic" and "obscene" materials with local communities.

19. An excellent statistical review of the ratio of divorce to marriage in the United States as well as several other nations is presented in Frank Cox, "Separation, Divorce, and Remarriage," cited in *American Marriage: A Changing Scene,* ed. Frank Cox (Dubuque, Iowa: William C. Brown, 1972), pp. 221–22.

20. Ibid., p. 223.

21. Leonard Benson, *The Family Bond: Marriage, Love, and Sex in America* (New York: Random House, 1971), p. 300.

22. Carl R. Rogers, "Man-Woman Relationships in the Year 2000," cited in Cox, *American Marriage,* pp. 246–47.

23. Atlee L. Stroup, "Are Marriage and the Family About to Disappear?" Ibid., p. 40.

24. Ibid.

25. Rogers, "Man-Woman Relationships in the Year 2000," p. 247.

26. Benson, *The Family Bond,* pp. 302 and 308.

27. Alvin Toffler, *Future Shock* (New York: Random House, 1970), cited in Cox, *American Marriage,* p. 168.

28. Ibid.

29. Vance Packard, *The Sexual Wilderness* (New York: David McKay, 1968), p. 284.

30. *Kansas City Star,* June 9, 1974.

31. Ibid., June 16, 1974.

32. Ibid.

33. Ibid.

34. "Alcoholism: New Victims, New Treatment," *Time,* April 22, 1974, p. 75.

35. Ibid.

36. Excellent insight into the recent decrease of heroin abuse among several segments of the population is presented by Robert L. Dupont, "The Rise and Fall of Heroin Addiction," *Natural History* 83, no. 6 (June-July 1974): 66–67.

37. *Kansas City Star,* June 16, 1974.

38. Eric Berne, *A Layman's Guide to Psychiatry and Psycho-Analysis* (New York: Ballantine Books, 1973), pp. 153–54.

39. Frank A. Goble, *The Third Force: The Psychology of Abraham Maslow* (New York: Pocket Books, 1974), p. 7.

40. Ibid., p. 121.

41. John A. Schindler, *How to Live 365 Days a Year* (Greenwich, Conn.: Fawcett Publications, 1968), p. 180.

42. Leonard Cammer, *Up From Depression* (New York: Pocket Books, 1971), pp. 12–13.

43. Ibid., p. 13.

44. Berne, *Layman's Guide to Psychiatry and Psycho-Analysis,* p. 136.

45. Ibid., p. 139.

46. Ibid., p. 171.

47. Ibid., p. 169.

48. Ibid., pp. 169–70.

49. Ibid., p. 170.

50. Ibid., p. 172.

51. Ibid., p. 177.

52. One of the most concise sources for introducing adolescents as well as adults to the phenomenon of human depression is Cammer, *Up From Depression,* p. 25.

53. Ibid., p. 26.

54. Ibid., p. 49.

55. Ibid., p. 55.

56. Ibid., p. 25.

57. Ibid., p. 173.

58. Ibid., pp. 184–85.

59. "Abortion and the Law," *New Republic* 170, no. 20 (May 18, 1974): 5.

60. Ibid., p. 6.

61. Ibid.

62. Euthanasia Educational Council, *Euthanasia* (New York, 1974).

63. W. R. Matthews, "Voluntary Euthanasia: The Ethical Aspect," cited in A. B. Downing, *Euthanasia and the Right to Death* (London: Peter Owen, 1971), p. 25.

64. One of the best current arguments for euthanasia, which can be readily understood by secondary students, is Marya Mannes, *Last Rights* (New York: William Morrow, 1974), p. 61.

65. Ibid., p. 62.

66. Carl Jay Bajema, "The Genetic Implications of Population Control," in Thomas Weaver, ed., *To See Ourselves: Anthropology and Modern Social Issues* (Glenview, Ill.: Scott, Foresman, 1973), p. 423.

67. Ibid., pp. 423–34.

68. Ibid., p. 424.

69. Ibid.

70. Ibid., p. 427.

71. Ibid., pp. 427–28.

72. Ibid., p. 428.

73. Ibid.

74. Ibid., pp. 428–29.

75. For an excellent discussion of the many social ramifications of modern eugenic theories, see L. C. Dunn, "Human Races: Genetic Factors," cited in *The Contemporary Scene,* ed. Paul B. Weisz (New York: McGraw-Hill, 1970), pp. 63–73 passim.

76. The continued decrease in the length of the work-week, in combination with the decrease in retirement ages during the last decade, has prompted this conclusion among many experts.

77. Donald O. Cowgill, "Aging in American Society," cited in *Aging and Modernization,* ed. Donald O. Cowgill and Lowell D. Holmes (New York: Appleton-Century-Crofts, 1972), pp. 243–45.

78. H. Dan Corbin and William J. Tait, *Education for Leisure* (Englewood Cliffs, N.J.: Prentice-Hall, 1973), pp. 4–6.

79. Cowgill, "Aging in American Society," p. 246.

80. Ibid.
81. Ibid., p. 244.
82. Ibid.
83. Ibid.
84. "These Missing Babies," *Time,* September 16, 1974, p. 62.
85. Ibid.
86. Ibid.
87. Ibid.
88. Cowgill, "Aging in American Society," p. 259.
89. Ibid., pp. 259–61.

CHAPTER 6

1. *Population Bulletin,* February 1971, pp. 11–12.
2. Ibid., October 1971, p. 7.
3. Ibid., p. 13.
4. Ibid., p. 15.
5. *Society Today* (Del Mar, Calif.: Communications Research Machines, 1971), p. 88.
6. Ibid., pp. 104–10.
7. Lloyd M. Jones, "Teaching about Urban Life in the Middle Grades," *Social Education* 33, no. 6 (October 1969): 75.
8. Yetta M. Goodman, "Metropolitan Man and the Social Studies," *Social Education* 33, no. 6 (October 1969): 700.
9. *Society Today,* pp. 104–5.
10. Lee Nelken Robins, "Social Problems Associated with Urban Minorities," cited in *Urban Life and Form,* ed. Werner Z. Hirsch. (New York: Holt, Rinehart, & Winston, 1963), p. 199.
11. Ibid., p. 203.
12. Ibid., p. 202.
13. *Society Today,* pp. 105–6.
14. Arnold W. Green, *Sociology: An Analysis of Life in Modern Society* (New York: McGraw-Hill, 1964), p. 206.
15. Ibid., p. 256.
16. United Press International, cited in *Wichita Eagle-Beacon,* June 12, 1974.
17. Andrew J. DuBrin, *Women in Transition* (Springfield, Ill.: Charles C. Thomas, 1972), p. 24.
18. Ibid.
19. Ibid., p. 25.
20. For evidence relating to the discrimination against women in American higher education, see *Chronicle of Higher Education,* Spring and Fall 1974, and Spring 1975. Excellent accounts of the many aspects of legal discrimination against women are presented in Karen DeCrow, *Sexist Justice* (New York: Random House, 1974), and Susan Deller Ross, *The Rights of Women* (New York: Avon Paperbacks, 1974).
21. For one of the most knowledgeable discussions of the causes and nature of criminality in the United States, see Ramsey Clark, *Crime in America* (New York: Simon & Schuster, 1970), p. 13 and pp. 35–43 passim.
22. Ibid., p. 17.
23. Ibid., pp. 56–62 passim.

24. James V. Panoch and David L. Barr, "Should We Teach about Religions in Our Public Schools?" *Social Education,* 33, no. 8 (December 1969): 910.

25. *Society Today,* p. 314.

26. Ibid.

27. Murray S. Stedman, Jr., *Religion and Politics in America* (New York: Harcourt, Brace & World, 1964), pp. 8–9.

28. Morris R. Lewenstein, *Teaching Social Studies in Junior and Senior High Schools* (Chicago: Rand McNally, 1963), pp. 50–51.

29. Randall C. Anderson, *Current Trends in Secondary School Social Studies* (Lincoln, Nebr.: Professional Educators Publications, 1972), pp. 16–17.

Bibliography

BANKS, JAMES A., ed. *Teaching Ethnic Studies.* 43rd Yearbook. Washington: National Council for the Social Studies, 1973. This is a book written by a group of distinguished scholars, both social and behavioral scientists and educators, who have devoted their professional careers to teaching about racial and ethnic problems in the United States. The entire publication is requisite for social studies teachers.

BENSON, LEONARD. *The Family Bond: Marriage, Love, and Sex in America.* New York: Random House, 1971. This book is designed to explore changing behavioral patterns through the human life-cycle from childhood and adolescence to maturity and old age. Parts 2, 3, and 4, which discuss adolescent relationships, marriage, and family deterioration, are particularly useful for social studies teachers.

BERGER, L., and BRIGITTE BERGER. *Sociology: A Biographical Approach.* New York: Basic Books, 1972. Since sociology represents the "core" of the secondary school behavioral science program, teachers would be advised to examine this book, which portrays the various thrusts that the discipline has taken in the United States during the contemporary period.

BERNE, ERIC. *A Layman's Guide to Psychiatry and Psycho-Analysis.* New York: Ballantine Books, 1973. Written by the author of *Games People Play,* this book provides a most perceptive insight into the mental illnesses of neurosis and psychosis, and progress in psychiatric treatment. Chapters 5, 6, and 8 are excellent sources for introducing topics on mental stress and illness to secondary students.

CAMMER, LEONARD. *Up From Depression.* New York: Pocket Books, 1971. In the opinion of the writer, this work represents one of the very best explanations of the causes, results, and potential cures for mental depression. Chapters 1 through 6 will provide social studies teachers with an excellent comprehension of depressive illness.

CLARK, RAMSEY. *Crime in America.* New York: Simon & Schuster, 1970. This work is perhaps the most authoritative examination of the many types of criminal behavior in the United States. A basic strength of the book is the manner in which the author analyzes criminal activities by socioeconomic groups in the nation. The entire book is highly recommended for social studies teachers.

CORBIN, H. DAN, and WILLIAM J. TAIT. *Education for Leisure.* Englewood Cliffs, N.J.: Prentice-Hall, 1973. The primary objective of this book is to promote leisure as a worthy vocation. The authors base their discussion on the premise that expanding leisure time and increasing materialistic affluence subject many individuals to overwhelming pressures which must be alleviated in the near future. Chapters 1 through 4 are particularly useful for secondary-age youth.

COWGILL, DONALD O., ed. *Aging and Modernization.* New York: Appleton-Century-Crofts, 1972. The authors examine the many problems, as well as the prospects, of older people in posttechnological societies like the United States, in underdeveloped societies, and in selected Communist nations. Chapters 16 through 19 provide valuable source material for the study of aging.

Cox, Frank, ed. *American Marriage: A Changing Scene.* Dubuque: William C. Brown, 1972. The contributors to this publication have done a remarkable job of discussing the changing patterns of marriage in the United States in relation to changes in other basic social institutions. Chapters 9 through 27 emphasize the future of marriage in our posttechnological society.

Du Brin, Andrew J. *Women in Transition.* Springfield, Ill.: Charles C. Thomas, 1972. This book provides a very good coverage of the contemporary development of the women's liberation movement in the United States. Chapters 1 through 5 provide excellent materials for presenting the significance of women's liberation to students.

Edwards, John N. *Sex and Society.* Chicago: Markham Publishing Co., 1972. The primary value of this book is found in the discussion of nonfamilial relationships, such as premarital sexual relations, homosexuality, and bisexuality. Chapters 2 through 7 provide excellent insight into these themes.

Ehman, Lee, Howard Mehlinger, and John Patrick. *Toward Effective Instruction in Secondary Social Studies.* Boston: Houghton Mifflin, 1974. This book on current social studies methods provides excellent source materials and strategies for teaching about political and social behavior. Chapter 6 emphasizes the formulation of inquiry-based techniques which can be utilized in grades seven through twelve.

Ehrlich, Paul R., and Anne H. Ehrlich. *Population, Resources, Environment: Issues in Human Ecology.* San Francisco: W. H. Freeman, 1970. All social studies teachers should be familiar with the thesis of this publication. It is invaluable as a reference for presenting the human consequences of overpopulation.

Feldman, Saul D., and Gerald W. Thielbar, eds. *Life Styles: Diversity in American Society.* Boston: Little, Brown, 1972. The authors present the many variations in American life-styles. Social studies instructors would find Chapters 3 through 10 particularly helpful in presenting "nontraditional" or controversial behavior patterns to secondary-age youth.

Fenton, Edwin. *Teaching the New Social Studies in Secondary Schools: An Inductive Approach.* New York: Holt, Rinehart & Winston, 1966. This book continues as the single most significant contribution to social education during the past decade. The role of the behavioral sciences in the social studies program is examined in detail in Chapter 23.

Green, Arnold W. *Sociology: An Analysis of Life in Modern Society.* 4th ed. New York: McGraw-Hill, 1964. The author examines the role of sociology as a behavioral science discipline in a very practical manner. In addition, he provides many examples of how sociologists contribute to the comprehension and solution of contemporary social problems.

Hirsch, Werner Z., ed. *Urban Life and Form.* New York: Holt, Rinehart & Winston, 1963. The authors provide excellent insight into the many and varied reasons why the recent phenomenon of urban growth in the United States continues to result in highly complex social problems. Chapters 6 through 9 are especially valuable.

Hollander, Edwin P. *Principles and Methods of Social Psychology.* New York: Oxford University Press, 1967. The author provides a thorough overview of the relatively new field of social psychology. Social studies teachers would be particularly interested in Chapters 1 and 2.

JUHASZ, ANNE, ed. *Sexual Development and Behavior: Selected Readings.* Homewood, Ill.: Dorsey Press, 1973. This should represent a basic source for teachers who are responsible for instruction in sex education since it analyzes the basic decisions that individuals must make when choosing a sexual life-style which is in harmony with self-concept, value systems, ideals, and aspirations. Chapters 1 through 12 are especially relevant for today's student.

KINCH, JOHN W., ed. *Social Problems in the World Today.* Reading, Mass.: Addison-Wesley, 1974. This recent publication discusses a wide range of social problems on a global basis. It is particularly useful for examining the changes in human behavior which have resulted from population growth and environmental depletion.

MANNES, MARYA. *Last Rights.* New York: William Morrow, 1974. The social, moral, religious, and legal ramifications of euthanasia are presented with great clarity in this book. Chapters 9, 10, 11, 12, and 13 should be familiar to all teachers responsible for introducing this controversial topic.

METCALF, LAWRENCE, ed. *Values Education: Rationale, Strategies, and Procedures.* 41st Yearbook. Washington: National Council for the Social Studies, 1971. This is one of the very best publications available today which emphasizes instructional procedures for teaching about value conflicts and value analysis, particularly Chapters 2 and 4.

National Academy of Sciences. *The Behavioral and Social Sciences: Outlook and Needs.* Englewood Cliffs, N.J.: Prentice-Hall, 1970. This entire book is absolutely vital for social studies teachers and curriculum planners who wish to integrate both method and content from the emerging behavioral sciences into the secondary social studies program.

————. *Resources and Man.* San Francisco: W. H. Freeman, 1969. Social studies instructors should find this publication an excellent source for portraying the necessity for mankind to alter its economic and social behavior in terms of the problem of environmental limitations.

POHLMAN, EDWARD, ed. *Population: A Clash of Prophets.* New York: New American Library, 1973. This is an invaluable source for teachers who wish to provide students with the awareness that many behavioral scientists believe that there is no problem of overpopulation on a global basis.

Population Bulletin. Washington: Population Reference Bureau. This bulletin is published monthly and represents the single best source for instructors who teach any aspect of population dynamics in social, political, or economic context.

TOFFLER, ALVIN. *Future Shock.* New York: Random House, 1970. A classic work on futuristics in terms of the changes that will influence life-styles and behavior in social, economic, and political perspective throughout the remainder of the twentieth century.

WEAVER, THOMAS, ed. *To See Ourselves: Anthropology and Modern Social Issues.* Glenview, Ill.: Scott, Foresman, 1973. Several of the nation's foremost anthropologists collaborated on this book to examine the emerging role of anthropology in the study of the human condition. Chapters 1, 2, 3, 5, and 6 are particularly beneficial for social studies teachers.

WEISZ, PAUL B. *The Contemporary Scene.* New York: McGraw-Hill, 1970. Social studies teachers would find Chapters 10, 11, and 12 particularly useful as a source of information for presenting topics which involve the individual and society, group interaction and society, and cultural values in terms of our changing society.

PB 68
25